INTRODUCTION TO BUSINESS TRANSLATION
A Handbook in English-Spanish
Contrastive Linguistics

Carmen Pérez Román
Francis Michel Ferrié

INTRODUCTION TO BUSINESS TRANSLATION
A Handbook in English-Spanish
Contrastive Linguistics

Second Revised and
Enlarged Edition

UPRED

EDITORIAL DE LA UNIVERSIDAD
DE PUERTO RICO
1993

First Edition, 1980
Second Edition, 1985, 1989,1993

Catalogación de la Biblioteca del Congreso
Library of Congress Cataloging-in-Publication Data

Pérez Román, Carmen
     Introduction to business translation.
     Bibliography: p.
     1. Bussines - Translating services. 2. English
     language - Business English. 3. English language -
     Translating into Spanish. 4. Spanish language -
     Business Spanish. 5. Spanish language -
     Translating into English.
I. Ferrié, Francis Michel. II. Title.
HF5351.P38   1985   428'.02   85-8581
ISBN 0-8477-3342-4

Impreso en los Estados Unidos de América
Printed in the United States of America

EDITORIAL DE LA UNIVERSIDAD DE PUERTO RICO
Apartado 23322
Estación de la U.P.R.
San Juan, Puerto Rico 00931-3322

FAX: (809) 751-8785

ACKNOWLEDGEMENTS

This 1985 edition of *Introduction to Business Translation* has retained its original purpose. It is dedicated to all the students of Business Communication we were priviliged to have in our classes. Their linguistics difficulties and their special needs have directed much of the matter here presented.

We are thankful to Professor Alejandro Bermúdez Avila, Department of Business English Chairperson, for his interest in the publication of this book.

Our appreciation also goes to Professors Angie A. Hill and Ana Irizarry Lamela, for their constructive criticism and encouragement.

We thank many of our colleagues who, each in special and valuable ways, have earned our gratitude.

TABLE OF CONTENTS

PREFACE 1

SOME METHODOLOGICAL CONSIDERATIONS 3

COURSE OBJECTIVES 7

TRANSLATION: SCOPE AND IMPORTANCE 8

TYPES OF TRANSLATION 11

FIGURATIVE LANGUAGE AND TRANSLATION 13

STEPS IN THE TRANSLATION PROCESS 14

UNITS

1. BUSINESS AND TECHNICAL TERMS 17

Part 1. English to Spanish 21
    2. Spanish to English 25
    3. Lexical Reinforcement Exercises
    (Spanish to English) 29

2. ENGLISH AND SPANISH IDIOMS 31

Part 1. English to Spanish 35
    2. Spanish to English 45
    3. Idiomatic Reinforcement Exercises
    (English to Spanish) 51

3. BUSINESS VOCABULARY ENRICHMENT
    (English to Spanish) 55

4. TRANSITIONAL EXPRESSIONS 61

Part 1. Functional Categories of Transitions 65
    2. Conjunctions: Coordinate, Subordinate
    and Correlative 71
    3. Application of Transitional Expressions
    (Spanish to English) 75

5. AUXILIARY VERBS IN INTERROGATIVE STRUCTURES 79

Part 1. Syntactical Comparison of English and Spanish
       Interrogative Forms 83
Part 2. Auxiliary verbs **to do** and **to have** 87
Part 3. Semantic Function of Modal Auxiliaries in
       English and Spanish Syntax 91
Part 4. Interrogative Words 95
Part 5. Use of There + Be as equivalent of Haber 97
Part 6. Reinforcement Exercises 99

6. COGNATES AND CONFUSING WORDS 105

Part 1. True Cognates 109
Part 2. Cognates with variation of meaning in Specific Contexts 111
Part 3. False Cognates 115
Part 4. Confusing Words 123
   5. Translation Exercises
     --Spanish to English 129
     --English to Spanish 130

7. PREPOSITIONS: FUNCTION AND APPLICATION 133

Part 1. English to Spanish 137
   2. English Equivalents 147
   3. Spanish to English 149
   4. Omission of Prepositions 153

8. TIME EXPRESSIONS 157

Part 1. Reinforcement Exercises in Question-Answer Form 161
    Prepositions Used with Expressions of Time 163
    Idioms (English to Spanish) 164
    Miscellaneous Expressions (Spanish) 166
    Technical Terms (English-Spanish) 167
    Nouns Expressing Time in various aspects 167
    FOR in Expressions of Duration of Time 168
Part 2. Spanish into English 169
Part 3. English into Spanish 171

9. COMPUTER TERMS 173

    Introduction 175
Part 1. Definitions in English and Spanish 177
Part 2. Sentences in English 183
Part 3. Computer, Data and Word Processing Terms in
       English and Spanish 185

GLOSSARIES 189

Part 1. English to Spanish 191
   2. Spanish to English 203

SELECTED REFERENCE BIBLIOGRAPHY 207

   Dictionaries 209

PREFACE

This book is a realistic attempt to meet the needs of those students for whom translation is indispensable for their vocational success. The selection and design of the material responds to common problems revealed by Spanish/English contrastive linguistics. Practical exercises in both languages are presented to develop the skills required for translating into both languages. The lexicon and style of these exercises, moreover, follow the patterns of contemporary business writing. While most of our students will be called upon to translate only the most straightforward of business communication forms (letters, memoranda, and short reports), our objective is to help them accomplish this task accurately and idiomatically in both English and Spanish.

Competency in both languages is expected from students who pursue this course. However, our experience testifies to the persistent language deficiencies that students bring to the classroom. To insure that they acquire minimum levels of proficiency in translation, emphasis is given specifically to contrastive analysis in the following three areas:

Lexicon: assimilation of the semantic content of common business vocabulary, especially English idiomatic expressions.

Structure: control of basic sentence patterns through recognizing the syntactical and grammatical differences involved in translating English and Spanish sentences.

Style: basic interpretative proficiency in selecting from among combinations of words and phrases those which best convey accuracy in meaning as well as appropriateness in nuance and tone.

With this objective in mind, therefore, our text establishes the priority on initiating students into the experience of translation first from English to Spanish. Linguistic theory and sound pedagogical practice support adopting the English to Spanish approach in the beginning stages.

Many translation scholars are convinced that to ensure complete competency in translating, the target language (that is, the language into which the text is to be rendered) should always be the translator's native language. Administrators of university graduate programs as well as

1

professional schools of translation uphold this opinion. These authorities insist that students be restricted to translating into the native language no matter how knowledgeable they may be of the foreign language they are converting. For this reason, candidates for admission to degree programs in translation must submit for evaluation examples of their writing in their native language. Because of the functional demands of the business world where the target language is primarily English, we cannot, however, limit the experience of translation to this ideal approach.

Emphasizing the native language as the target language in the introductory phase of translation learning is constructive. It serves to familiarize the student with correct linguistic structures of the foreign language immediately. Since English, at this stage, is the weaker language for the majority of our students, they need to be presented, from the outset, with model sentence forms. In this way, they develop an awareness of proper word order, correct grammar, spelling, and punctuation, before being faced with material for translation into English. To have to grapple with poorly translated English copy in the initial phase deprives students of the opportunity to absorb English structural patterns so fundamental for meaning to be fully understood and accurately communicated.

The preference for initiating the translation process with exercises from English to Spanish holds a distinct psychological advantage. Students have an uncounscious, intuitive control of syntax as well as wider range of lexical content in their native language. Moreover, they are usually well acquainted with the characteristics of formal and informal native language styles. Translation from English to Spanish is simply easier for them because they are not hampered unnecessarily with foreign linguistic patterns they sometimes do not fully recognize, much less control. This approach builds confidence, and every language teacher knows the importance of early success.

As a reinforcement activity, therefore, this translation course consolidates work in other linguistic areas of the Business Communication curriculum. The levels of proficiency in Spanish and English will, of course, determine to a great extent the pace of improvement in acquiring translation skills. Some perplexing difficulties will always persist for second-language learners. Certainly, greater competency in translation can only be assured when students attain higher degrees of mastery of the native language. Such a goal lies well beyond the scope of this simple and unpretentious handbook, however, our hopes are much more modest: that the contents of this introductory text, incorporating the insights of contrastive linguistics, will improve the command of Spanish and English already achieved by our students so that the task of translation will become for them a little less burdensome.

SOME METHODOLOGICAL CONSIDERATIONS

Translation, by its very nature, is a painstaking and laborious activity. This is all the more true of business translation, where the purpose is generally functional and the context often predictable. While the student's level of language competency has dictated in great measure the content and arrangement of this handbook, creativity and imagination must be applied in using the material included. Without incorporating these facets into the translation process, we, teachers, run the risk of provoking perfunctory and apathetic responses from our students. The task of making the translation course an enjoyable learning experience, therefore, falls squarely on the shoulders of the instructor.

Every instructor brings his own special blend of talents and skills as well as methodological insights to the translation course. We would like to share with you some methods we considered particularly valuable to demonstrate how the material of the text can be creatively used. These methodological adaptations that follow are not exclusive, nor are they intended to direct, in any way, the teaching approach of this course. They are offered simply as examples of imaginative application of method to a course content (series of selected sentences) with emphasis on realistic objectives (reinforcement of lexicon, structures, and style common to business writing) that might otherwise be viewed by both students and instructors as mechanical, and therefore, monotonous.

1) The Cloze Test

Originally a method used to test the levels of reading comprehension of native speakers, it has since been adopted as a popular model for measuring achievement and proficiency of second-language learners. In the "Cloze" technique, a passage is selected from which words are deleted intermittently (perhaps, the 5th, 6th, or 7th). Students must supply other acceptable words to fit the context. Deletions should not be limited to one type of grammatical or lexical form, but should represent a wide variety of semantic elements-auxiliary components of the main verb, nouns, adjectives, adverbial phrases, transitional words, etc. Spanish substitutes can be supplied for complete English deletions, or vice versa.

Instructors may adapt the material of the text to practice this technique, or bring to class original material from business magazines, reviews, as well as newspaper commentaries on local business transactions, etc. The benefit of the "Cloze technique" permits the students to discriminate in choosing the most appropriate word or phrase to fit the context. Since there may well be more than one acceptable substitute, this method helps the student to concentrate on the context itself for meaning rather than on one or other particular lexical item. Student translators begin to "listen" better so as to capture the tone of the passage and the nuances suggested by the writer. In this way, the translation activity can be appreciated as an interpretative medium.

2) The Pattern-drill Concept

This conversational language technique might be adopted occasionally to help those students who are weak in the use of vocabulary and the knowledge of structural patterns. The lexicon and structure of one of the model sentences can be varied, beginning with minor adaptations and continuing with more complex changes, as the abilities of the students permit. It seems best to begin with simple structural changes: principal verb tense changes; verb tense changes affecting verbs in subordinate clauses; verb tense changes adding appropriate adverbial phrases; verb tense changes utilizing modal auxiliaries with appropriate phrasal variations; verb substitutes. After the basic structure of the sentence has been adequately reinforced, noun and adjective substitutions might then be made. While minor adaptations and simple substitutions can be orally translated, more complex structural changes would have to be dictated so that students can translate them in writing. These more complex changes would include: active to passive voice, and vice versa declarative to interrogative form, etc.

3) Lexical enrichment through derivational prefixes and suffixes

One of the most effective vocabulary enrichment exercises is the recognition and practice of contrastive prefixes and suffixes, especially those which have similar linguistic roots in both languages. Prefixes, both in meaning and form, are relatively fixed in both languages and should pose no difficulty for students, for example: anti- / auto- / neo- / con- / contra- / pro- / re- / semi- / sub- / super- / trans- / (circum- / circun-) (post- / pos-) (un- / in- o des-). As regards the more difficult suffixes, the instructor might point out the most productive and less unambiguous of noun, verb, and adjectival derivational markers to begin: nouns from nouns, -ism-ismo; -ist-ista; nouns from adjectives, -cy-cia, -ity-idad; adjectives from nouns, -al-al, ic-ico, -ous(-oso, -es); adjectives from verbs, -able-able, -ent-ente, -ive-ivo, -ary-ario, -ed(-ado, -ido); verbs

4

from nouns and adjective - ize-izar, ate-ar, -fy-ficar. The derivational variants lead the students to isolate those suffixes peculiary native to English: -er, -ness, -ful, -ly, -less, -y, -wise, -ward(s), -ster, -ship, -ish. While this technique of vocabulary enrichment might be used to amplify the unit on cognates, the lexical examples can be taken from those used in various units of the text, especially the first unit. In this way, the roots of the words studies in the vocabulary can be utilized to reinforce lexicon and develop translation flexibility: for example, when words are presented in the units as verbs (convey), they can be changed into adjectives and nouns (conveyor, conveyance).

4) Lexical research projects

Business lexicon increasingly has to accept new concepts, applications and technologies brought about by rapid change. New words and phrases are coined repeatedly to define new conceptual and technical experiences (terms, for example, common to more than one area of business - allocation / apportionment / deployment / divesture / forecasting / feedback / interfacing / network: and various technical combinations - capital asset pricing / common stock evaluation models / document feed / electrical outage / inflated price issue / methods time measurement / performance appraisal systems / process layout / weighted average earnings / zero-based budgeting). These new terms make it more difficult for the business expert to communicate his ideas to the layman. The translator, therefore, must continually update his knowledge of vocabulary in the diverse areas of business and seek corresponding referents in the native language to render meaning adequately. Consequently, student translators might be given the task of compiling specialized word lists to express new semantic developments. The instructor might ask students to seek in different organizational departments (finance, marketing, sales, production, personnel, corporate legal, etc.) a list of contemporary terms and expressions used in communication material as well as in current articles and textbooks in the different fields of business. This review of lexical usage will help them to identify common and idiomatic expressions peculiar to the business environment. Such material can be brought to class to incorporate in sentences for translation.

5) Selection and use of supplementary material for translation practice

The practice of introducing short selections in English and in Spanish for translation in class is highly recommended. These selections, usually of two or three paragraphs in length, might be culled from the business section of newspapers and/or from business magazines, periodical and reports. In this way, students can be exposed to the contextual variety of up-to-date topics and language of the contemporary business world. Such selections, moreover, will help to enhance the quality of the material offered in the text, thus making the learning process more pedagogically appealing and more personally satisfying to all concerned.

5

Obviously, the passages chosen by the instructor will need to be carefully reviewed and then graded for increasing levels of difficulty.

The method to be employed in translating the selections should simulate as closely as possible the experience of the translator under the various pressures of a real-life situation. We envision this method as follows. Students should attempt a quick draft of the selected material with the emphasis on communicating meaning. At this stage, a dictionary should not be used; rather, they should be encouraged to be as inventive as possible in rendering the best contextual translation without any external aids whatsoever. This practice helps the students to see where their particular difficulties lie and allows the instructor to deal spontaneously with common problems as they arise. When the initial draft is completed, a dictionary can then be used to check to verify the accuracy of lexical choice so as to avoid ambiguity in communicating the meaning intended. A second draft can then be made with attention given to matters of fluency and style.

Students should be advised to adopt this method as an habitual approach to any translation task. Besides helping them to pinpoint individual difficulties, it will allow them to chart more systematically their individual progress. Before the end of the translation course, two complete articles, one in Spanish and the other in English, might be offered to the students as a profitable home assignment. A review of their accomplishment of this exercise should help to increase their confidence in confronting the demands of a lengthy business topic.

COURSE OBJECTIVES

The objectives for this course are both general and specific. The former share the purpose of any language-training course in that they offer valid but relatively unquantifiable results; the latter, on the other hand, can be progressively measured and tested.

GENERAL

1. To help the student develop a discriminating judgement of the nature and function of language.

2. To make students aware of the academic value of the discipline of translation in fostering their own intellectual development and cultural growth.

3. To make students aware of the important role translation plays in promoting understanding among peoples since particular idioms tend to embody cultural views and atttitudes peculiarly their own.

SPECIFIC

1. To familiarize the student with the basic principles of translation as these apply to communication in general and to business communication in particular.

2. To acquaint the student with idiomatic expressions used in business and everyday language, enabling them to understand and communicate in English with greater fluency and precision.

3. To emphasize the differences in structure between English and Spanish, thus improving accuracy in communicating meaning.

4. To encourage the students to utilize the tools and resources available for the most accurate contextual translation (especially dictionaries).

5. To encourage the students to increase their working knowledge of professional and technical terminology in both Spanish and English.

TRANSLATION: SCOPE AND IMPORTANCE

Translation is important both from the sociological and the intellectual viewpoints. It bridges the gap between diverse cultural backgrounds and social systems. Moreover by loosening the bonds of misunderstanding, translation is a vehicle for effective exchange of ideas as well as a means of fostering cultural contacts. Competence in translating helps to promote reciprocity, cooperation, empathy and rapport among peoples.

Translators must have broad cultural backgrounds. They must be like sponges constantly soaking up knowledge of all kinds. An effective translator must be aware that ideas in one language may have no equivalent referent in another; that apparent meanings can many times be misleading. A translator's ability to interpret, therefore, demands not only a heavy dose of common sense, but also a keen sensitivity to language nuance. Mutual understanding, indeed, may rest on this ability.

The basis for effective translation is a knowledge of syntax. It is absolutely essential to bring out the intended meaning of the context and to insure freedom from distortion and ambiguity.

Let's look at a common difficulty in syntaxis for translators working with both English and Spanish. Notice for example, the position of the noun adjectives in both English and Spanish forms that follow:

price list	lista de *precios*
list *price*	*precio* de lista
cane sugar	azúcar de *caña*
sugar *cane*	*caña* de azúcar
tower clock	reloj *de la torre*
clock *tower*	*torre* del reloj
filter paper	papel de *filtro*
paper *filter*	*filtro* de papel

We might say therefore that when two nouns in English are associated, one must translate into Spanish the second noun first.

Otherwise, the meaning intended changes when the order is inverted. Without knowing the syntactical peculiarity, misinterpretation is inevitable.

Let's look at another example. In phrases having two modifiers plus a substantive, the translator should translate into Spanish, in inverse order as:

effective-communication channels	canales de *comunicación efectiva*
group-insurance program	programa de *seguro grupal*
long-wave reception	recepción de *onda larga*
profit-sharing program	programa de *participación de beneficios*

Another fundamental for avoiding misunderstanding in the translation process is a close reading of the meaning of the text. This is specially true when words have multiple meanings. Notice the examples below:

Invierta el orden de la oración.	*Invert* the word order in the sentence.
Invierta dinero en este proyecto.	*Invest* money in this project.
El motor de la *bomba* de agua está averiado.	The motor of the water *pump* is out of order.
Los rebeldes colocaron una *bomba* en un edificio del gobierno.	The rebels placed a *bomb* in a government building.
Take her to the hospital when her *labor pains* start.	Llévela al hospital cuando le empiecen sus *dolores de parto.*
At present, *labor unions* are powerful.	Actualmente, los *sindicatos obreros* son poderosos.
Labor cost is rising at gigantic speed.	El *costo de la mano de obra* está subiendo a paso gigantesco.
They *labor* hard to achieve their goal.	Ellos *trabajan* fuerte para alcanzar su meta.

Many languages are full of words with multiple meanings. Therefore, intelligent use of dictionaries is a necessity. Of course, dictionaries do not tell everything about a word. Often the words used in the context to be translated are not used in their dictionary meaning at all, but in a connotative or figurative sense.

In the sentence: "The country was ribboned with cement highways," the translator has to know the meaning of the concept ribbon. Therefore, in Spanish, the sentence is translated as fallows: "El país estaba encintado de carreteras;" "El país tenía un sinnúmero de carreteras."

Knowledge of synonyms is also important because they secure a pleasing variety in the translator's mode of expression. However, true synonyms are rare in most languages. But the translator should be knowledgeable enough to determine which words have characteristics in common to fit the meaning, tone, and rhythm of the passage he is translating.   Technology has shrunk distances, thus facilitating international communication. There is a pressing need for qualified language specialists capable of meeting the demands of modern business, science, politics, art, and society in general. Professionals mastering multilingual communication are an asset anywhere and doors are automatically open for them.

TYPES OF TRANSLATION

The function of effective translation is the careful rendering of ideas into another language. To accomplish this task successfully, the translator must be aware of three types of translation.

THE LITERAL TRANSLATION: where the translator gives word for word, the equivalent meaning of the terms in the original. Therefore the meaning is subordinate to the word; that is, the meaning depends on the specific word that is used. This type of translation is valuable when studying the differences in syntax and idiom between two languages. It is also advocated when one encounters difficulty in translating a passage in literary form.

Example: Estaba todo arreglado y preparado de antemano, de modo que la reunión fue innecesaria.

All was arranged and prepared for beforehand; therefore the meeting was unnecessary.

THE LITERARY TRANSLATION : where the meaning of the original is closely followed, but rendered according to the idomatic characteristics of the language. Thus, the translation will be characterized by a smooth idiomatic flow. There are different degrees of literary translation; however. In creative and artistic literary works, style is personal and must oftentimes be given as much importance as meaning with which it is intimately connected. In business, industrial and government writings, style is functional, and therefore secondary to meaning. For the purposes of this book, keep in mind that business translation emphasizes the communication of meaning.

smooth idiomatic flow

style + meaning or meaning + style

Example: Estaba todo arreglado y preparado de antemano de modo que la reunión fue innecesaria.

Everything was arranged and agreed upon beforehand; therefore, it was unnecessary to hold the meeting.

THE FREE TRANSLATION: where the language and style of the original are not at all strictly followed. The translator simply attempts to convey the important ideas of the original. This is a very difficult task. In order to translate so freely a translator must be thoroughly conversant with the language, culture and thought of the original.

Example: Estaba todo arreglado y preparado de antemano.

Everything was cut and dried, so we didn't need to meet.

FIGURATIVE LANGUAGE AND TRANSLATION

The style of effective business writing is characterized by simplicity and clarity. Such characteristics do not exclude the use of figurative language in business copy. In fact, advertising and sales letters often resort to rhetorical figures to achieve their persuasive aims.

Figurative language, when properly applied, creates pictorial images which add life and vigor to the written and spoken word. The business translator, therefore, should be familiar with the more common rhetorical figures so as to convert them correctly.

Some figures of speech are the following:

The Simile: Two dissimilar objects are compared by the use of like or as.

Notice the similes in this excerpt from a business report of the Westinghouse Electric Corporation. "The most delicate meters made by Westinghouse use wire like strands of gossamer: 0008 of an inch in diameter, or about one fourth as thick as a human hair. The wheels turn on pivots ten times as sharp as a sewing needle."

The Metaphor: There is an implied comparison between objects of unlike classes.

"Sincere friendship is one of the greatest investments in the market of life. He who tries to become a millionaire over the short haul through the manipulation of friendship, on the other hand, will not be affected by the rise and fall of life's misfortunes."

Personification: An object, idea, or animal is given human attributes.

1) During the sixties, inflation raised its ugly head.
2) Money is the mistress of power.
3) With the rise in oil prices, the OPEC nations have given birth to a multiheaded monster.

STEPS IN THE TRANSLATION PROCESS

The translation process now forms such an integral part of the international business scene that students must become aware of the skills translation demands. It is neither fully an art, nor fully a science, yet combines elements of both. No translator can hope to contribute to the success of a business enterprise without continually developing both the technical and artistic requirements that effective translation entails.

Students are not sufficiently experienced to translate a text at first glance. Yet it is a habit they frequently indulge in. To launch oneself into the difficult task of rendering someone else's thoughts into another language without careful preparation can lead to serious blunders.

The initial step calls for a complete reading of the original text. From this reading the translator comprehends the essence of the writer's thought. Moreover, the translator, like the business communicator, should establish a sense of empathy with the writer which enables him to get the feeling of the ideas stated. It is the meaning of the whole that must be conveyed rather than the meaning of the parts.

Obviously if the original contains any error in grammar or syntax, the translator must then make the pertinent corrections before proceeding with the translation. In matters of style, many times the translator has to recast a whole passage to communicate meaning accurately. Before attempting to do so, however, the translator must always consult the author.

While recasting is generally a permissive practice in translations, the beginning student translator should realize that his efforts may be jeopardized by straying too far from the original subject matter. In other words, what should be uppermost in the mind of the translator is that he must be a bridge between the author and the readers.

The next step is the writing of the draft. A draft is not a final copy. Students must avoid the careless habit of considering their first copy as final. Usually, the results are inferior to acceptable standards. There are several ways of expressing an idea, and the first attempt at translating it may not be the best.

After editing the draft, the translator may write the finished copy. A polished translation, therefore, should be characterized by the following:

1. Complete faithfulness to the original when rendering the idea.

2. Observance of word order. Thus, the translator will show that he understands perfectly the structure of both languages he is working with.

3. Observance of the principles of style. Thus, endeavoring to give the readers the nuance and tone they would have had if they had read the original.

Steps

1. Complete reading of original text
2. Comprehend essence of the writer thoughts.
3. get the feeling of the ideas stated (tone)
4. Write a draft. (look up words etc.)
5. Edit the draft (language structure & style/tone)
6. Finalize the translation (Smooth idiomatic flow)
   a. faithful to original (accurate meaning)
   b. Word order - language structure
   c. Style and tone faithful to original

UNIT I
BUSINESS AND TECHNICAL TERMS

Part 1   English to Spanish

Part 2   Spanish to English

Part 3   Lexical Reinforcement Exercises
               Spanish to English

BUSINESS AND TECHNICAL TERMS

The translation exercises which follow are typical of the vocabulary and style of contemporary business written expression. You will translate first the English sentences into Spanish giving particular attention to the underlined technical words and phrases. Then, you will translate the Spanish sentences into English. Even though English is the international business language, translation into English should be attempted only after you have sufficient practice translating from English to Spanish.

The terms in italics in the examples which follow are, of course, only a representative selection to help familiarize you with the type of language common to various businesses and related fields. As you tackle the translation, you should keep the following observations in mind:

-- No real development in translation skills can be achieved by simply deciphering each unknown word with the aid of a dictionary or the special wordlist we facilitate for you in this text. No amount of knowledge of technical terms can be combined to communicate meaning until the sentence structures, which carry the meaning, are clearly understood.

-- Once you have learned the meaning of the technical words and phrases in their specific context (that is, as part of the complete meaning of the sentence), you will be able to convey the intended idea accurately. If further difficulties persist, your instructor will identify the source of misinterpretation and clarify any remaining problems.

PART 1
ENGLISH TO SPANISH

Read the sentence as a whole before translating it. Watch verb tense and syntax.

1. The cashier at the supermarket *alienated* the customers by her poor service and discourteous attitude.

2. My professor studied in New York University where he *earned a degree* in political science in May, 1980.

3. I will invest the *accrued interest* on the *promissory note* in new municipal bonds.

4. Please fill out this evaluation form; it will let us know *how we rate* among first-class hotels.

5. I had to *defray the costs* of graduate study by *auditing* the steel company's *books* for two successive summers.

6. A corporate lawyer who was *admitted to the bar* five years ago, is facing *disbarment* for unethical practices.

7. The committee *laid out their plans* early for the *appropriation of funds* for the proposed housing project for the aged.

8. The federal judge instructed the *defendant* to post bail on a charge of *contempt of court.*

9. The *referee in bankruptcy* explained that the company went bankrupt because of *bad debts* and administrative inefficiencies.

10. The brochure we are enclosing outlines the advantages of using wood *by-products.* Since we *carry on business* with several of your domestic concerns, you may check with them about the *gratifying results* they have had in dealing with us.

11. My car needs a proper checkup by a *qualified* mechanic.

12. Because of poor trade, the dealer *bargained away* 25% of the *costume jewelry* and cancelled plans *to replenish his stock.*

13. The cost accountant is concerned about our exaggerated *upkeep* and *overhead* expenses and advises us to *cut* them *in half.*

14. *Don't underrate* the power of the unions to get what they want.

15. This corporation appreciates the *courtesies* extended our agent when he was trying to register our *firm name* in your country.

16. The *department head* of our dairy explained that it costs more to package milk in *cardboard containers* than in bottles.

17. The trend nowadays is for companies to seek a *merger rather than to change hands.*

18. The Board of Directors gave the General Manager *carte blanche* to develop a plan that would *answer the needs* of the company employees.

19. *Far-reaching measures* to cut down traffic jams - a *pressing matter for everyone - were the spokesman's opening statements* that drew the loudest applause.

20. Frequent strikes in any country are one of the principal *drawbacks to economic progress.*

21. *A well-prepared schedule* will *expedite* our varied activities. Besides it will help to *cut down* our *running expenses.*

22. The *price ceilings* on *staples* might soon increase considerably.

23. Because of the policemen's *oversight* when *filing the charge,* the accused was not convicted.

24. It might be *feasible* to devise a plan to eliminate the *flaws* and *bottlenecks* in our supply department.

25. The *appraiser* has authority to make a thorough and correct valuation of property of any kind.

26. In order to *figure out* in advance the prices *to quote* on appliances sold on a cash basis, *please forward the goods early.*

27. *The salesman's well-timed visit* gave me a chance to discuss the controversial *freight charges* that are constantly *holding up* our orders.

28. Before *filling the order* for home delivery, check if the *freight expenses* are included in the price.

29. I am unable to tell you *from memory* which of our *white-collar* employees enjoy a sizeable *take-home pay.*

30. Though they *jeopardized* their lives, the *maintenance crews* went immediately to the scene of the disaster.

31. The United States Congress now has power to *freeze ceiling prices* in order *to curb inflation.*

32. *The newspaper announced that HUD will subsidize* the mortgage payments of some of the home buyers.

33. That firm is very prompt to answer the requests of *would-be* clients.

34. *Sort out* the merchandise and send it to Mr. Rivera. However, put pressure on him so that he settles his *outstanding account* without our having to take legal action.

35. *Wholesalers* must take into account the cost of keeping merchandise in inventory; *retailers,* on the other hand, must take into account the cost of keeping the inventory *on hand.*

36. The *van* from the moving company should pick up the furniture today so as *to be in time* for the Navieras' sailing schedule.

37. The *likelihood* that prices may be increased to match *rising costs* will be a big blow to *export companies.*

38. The latest *developments* underscore the need for granting substantial *quantity discounts* to the packaging company. Otherwise, they will look for a better deal.

39. We are *out of stock* on small electronic calculators. Why don't we buy them form Carribbean Computers that is *liquidating* its business?

40. The *purchasing power of the consumer* is generally affected by world politics.

41. The striking dock workers were *reluctant* to unload even *perishable foodstuffs* badly needed by hospitals and rest homes.

42. *Cobol,* a computer language, is very popular and easy to learn.

43. The methods the marketing manager helped *pioneer* have eliminated distribution *bottlenecks.*

44. The report concluded that the *rate of exchange* would affect the total profit to be *realized* by the transaction.

45. The substandard conditions of the premises oblige us to *move out* and to demand from you *to refund* our *down-payment.*

46. The *rise and fall* of the market prevents us from *quoting prices* on next summer's sports clothes.

47. Because the flood destroyed the harvest, the farmer could not *meet* his *quarterly payment.* Consequently, he will probably not be able *to settle his account* that *matures* at the end of the year.

48. Because of the shortage *forced upon us,* ask our customer if he will accept a substitute for Item 4, before we *release the order.*

49. He *contends* that even though we are getting suitable prices, the *large stock on hand* does not justify ordering additional merchandise.

50. Since the sales manager *merits* your confidence, give him the power of attorney to claim the $1,000 involved in the *stale* check.

51. The *staple* food for the majority of Puerto Rican families is rice and beans.

52. We are *out of stock* on those articles just now because they have been *held up* at the docks. We have been assured, however, that our supply *will be replenished* next week.

53. For an accurate *appraisal* of the situation, take stock of all *dormant merchandise* before straightening out the accounts.

54. The Telephone Company does not accept reservations for ads after the April *deadline*.

55. *Don't throw money away* by sending that old equipment in *tamper-proof containers*. Nothing will go *wrong* by shipping it surface mail in cardboard boxes.

56. On account of the incorrect *tally of votes* to select the union representative for dealing with members crossing the picket line, we must *contest* the election. After that, we can present a qualified candidate.

57. Some socialist countries *have voided* Christmas as an official holiday.

58. This check *is void* because the date has been erased.

59. The rise in oil prices *has brought about* world-wide inflation.

60. *Reluctantly*, the investor *withdrew* his support from the project. His financial advisor made him believe our *domestic* and foreign investments are in *jeopardy*.

61. A company having *foreign* markets is better off than the one that has *domestic* markets only.

62. Because of the wild *scramble* for the merchandise in the docks, the mediator *yielded* to the terms.

63. *Underselling* practices and inflated prices are detrimental to local industry.

64. Our company has been holding *quartely* management meetings since last year.

65. When the acting manager *resigned,* he received a lump sum of $10,000 because of *accrued vacation*, sick leave and other fringe *benefits.

PART 2
SPANISH TO ENGLISH

Before translating the following sentences, be sure to read them carefully to grasp content and to check verb tense.

1. El banco no *honró* el cheque porque la cuenta estaba *sobregirada*.

2. *La noticia sobre la venta inminente* de nuestra compañía se *filtró* ayer.

3. Su actitud *loable* influyó en que se efectuara la repartición de la herencia sin más dilación.

4. Si a los dos empleados no se les *reinstala en su puesto, el grupo sentará* argumentos convincentes (fuertes) para irse a la huelga.

5. La decisión del juez está *sujeta a apelación* en la corte federal.

6. Los *estibadores* se quejaron de que no había inspectores para *cotejar la carga.*

7. *Abrogar* una ley significa revocarla, es decir, dejarla sin efecto.

6. Según la situación, el *inventario inicial* no revelará nada que ellos no hayan predicho ya.

9. En su informe de *entradas* y gastos (estado de situación), él manifestó que las ganancias de la compañía están en *proporción* a los aumentos de inversiones.

10. *Mantenga en el archivo* una lista *detallada (desglosada) de los problemas que encaramos (afrontamos) debido a la merma (baja) en la venta de productos congelados.*

11. *El llevar un récord* cuidadoso de los datos sobre la *vivienda subvencionada* por el gobierno en la zona urbana, minimizará los problemas.

12. No *subestime* la importancia del programa sobre *mercados extranjeros* que se presentará mañana por televisión.

13. Los huelguistas deben *darse cuenta* que entre los víveres detenidos en los muelles, hay furgones llenos de *artículos de primera necesidad* que se necesitan con urgencia en los comedores escolares.

14. No tenemos *existencia* de maquinaria pesada por ahora, pero esperamos surtirnos la próxima semana.

15. Asegúrese de que ni los anuncios ni las *etiquetas* de precios sean *engañosos*.

16. *El gobierno impone contribuciones altas* al licor y a los cigarrillos.

17. Aunque su ingreso personal haya aumentado considerablemente este año, *reduzca* sus *gastos* porque el *poder adquisitivo* del dólar varía mucho.

18. Debemos apresurarnos y *solicitar respaldo* para nuestra investigación de mercadeo antes de que mermen los fondos de la compañía.

19. Al abogado *se le designó* para testificar en la vista sobre la conveniencia de construir una *estación de gasolina* en esa área.

20. A *corta distancia* del accidente pudimos observar un gran *contingente* de policías que obligaba a los *espectadores* a retroceder.

21. Usualmente, *la fecha límite* para enviar correspondencia de Navidad al Lejano Oriente es el primero de diciembre.

22. El orador le *cedió la palabra* a su colega, quien deseaba traer a colación un asunto que tenía que resolverse inmediatamente.

23. El traslado de nuestro talentoso gerente ha dejado un *vacío* en nuestra sucursal.

24. El metanol, que es un *derivado* del carbón, probablemente se podrá usar como cumbustible en los automóviles.

25. La inundación que *azotó* a los agricultores hace unos meses, ha sido su peor *revés* en muchos años.

26. Creemos que el plan para *subvencionar* los costos de manutención de las familias de bajos ingresos es *factible*.

27. *Entre los empleados de cuello azul* de la industria automotriz hay muchos mecánicos diestros.

28. El dividendo *trimestral* de 75¢ por acción se les pagará a todos los tenedores de acciones.

29. El tenedor de libros *rastreó el error* y lo encontró en una de las columnas del *balance de comprobación*.

30. El rápido *deterioro natural* de nuestra maquinaria ha creado un problema económico difícil para nosotros.

31. Haga un informe sobre los tres empleados cuyas obligaciones estamos *subvencionando* y de quienes creemos que *gastan más de lo que ganan*.

32. El *comité de escrutinio* informó que 75% de los miembros había votado en contra de extender por dos años más el término de funciones al señor Rosa.

33. La Comisión de Derechos hace lo mejor posible para que el gobierno reconozca la importancia de *poner en vigor* leyes que eviten que se *coarten* los derechos del individuo.

34. La nota *devenga* un interés tan elevado que el *corredor de bienes raíces* aconsejó a su cliente que estudiase su decisión cuidadosamente.

35. La compañía solía *tener en existencia* muchos *artículos de marcas conocidas que ya no se encuentran en el mercado.*

36. *Al pagar la deuda,* por favor solicíteles un *estado detallado* de los *cargos de aduana* que nos han cobrado durante los últimos dos meses.

37. Prepare planes *de contingencia* para nosotros poder afrontar la emergencia, porque la situación tiene todas las características de una huelga prolongada.

38. El estar ellos *en desgracia* coloca a estos empleados en una posición difícil en lo que concierne a su propuesta.

39. Por si el *aviso de cobro* que le enviamos se ha *extraviado,* le estamos enviando un duplicado.

40. El periodista declaró que se le habían *coartado* sus derechos al no dejarle expresar su opinión.

PART 3

LEXICAL REINFORCEMENT EXERCISES
(Spanish to English)

Translate the following sentences as accurately as possible. Prepare a list of the terms that are completely new to you.

1. El *hacinamiento* en las cárceles *pone en peligro* la salud física y la emocional de los *reclusos*.

2. La Junta de la Reserva Federal parece estar *aflojando su política de austeridad* (estrechez) *monetaria*.

3. *No favorecemos la congelación* de los fondos que hay disponibles para *subvencionar* viviendas a bajo costo.

4. El señor Rivera no nos acreditó el cheque porque el mismo *había sido emitido hace seis meses.*

5. *El salario de estos empleados potenciales para trabajo de investigación será en proporción a su experiencia.* En su *solicitud de empleo*, notamos que ellos han contribuído grandemente al estudio de áreas productivas para *inversiones.*

6. El señor Ríos, supervisor de tránsito, se retira el próximo mes. Su retiro *dejará un vacío* en nuestra institución. Además de su excelente labor en su departamento, sus aportaciones a otras áreas de servicio público son *dignas de encomio.*

7. Como le estamos comprando cien docenas de sobres impresos, le agradeceremos nos *conceda un descuento mayor por comprar en grandes cantidades.*

8. *Sin lugar a dudas*, la policía *siguió la pista del fugitivo* de una manera inteligente. También es digno de encomio como ellos *pusieron lo mejor de su parte* para *soportar las agrias dificultades* causadas por personas que no deseaban cooperar.

9. Dos de nuestros accionistas son candidatos para puestos políticos. Al ejercer tu voto, debes *tomar una decisión* inteligente: no prestar atención a rumores infundados y seleccionar aquellos *prospectos* que a tu juicio *no faltarán a su palabra* una vez sean electos.

10. Un ejecutivo de la compañía petrolífera desea *abrir una cuenta con nosotros*. Sin embargo, hemos sabido que tiene varias *cuentas*

pendientes con otras casas comerciales. *De momento,* no tengo los nombres de estas casas pero te los daré tan pronto los consiga. *Bajo ningún concepto* esta información debe *trascender.*

11. El presidente de la empresa le dió *un poder* al *analista de finanzas* para efectuar la transacción. No pude acompañarle a la oficina del abogado porque tenía que resolver *un asunto importante* relacionado con el *horario de los empleados a tarea parcial* y el *reembolso de los gastos* de viaje del gerente interino.

12. El señor Ramos, *juez de quiebras,* fue miembro de la junta ejecutiva de nuestra compañía. En la reunión pasada, él *impugnó el informe del comité de escrutinio* y al discutirse el asunto se *trajo a colación* una pléyade de asuntos desagradables. Sin embargo, el señor Ramos presentó *argumentos* muy *convincentes* para apoyar su acción.

13. Debido a la *huelga que se avecina,* estamos *afrontando una situación crítica,* ya que *no tenemos muchos víveres.* Algunos de los *productos* que escasean son de *primera necesidad* y todavía el gobierno no les ha *fijado los precios máximos.* Si el gobierno no toma alguna acción *dentro de unos días,* estamos seguros que habrá especulación con estos artículos.

14. Nos interesa estar listos para *afrontar contingencias* antes que el *tipo de cambio* varíe drásticamente. Al efecto, estamos preparando un *presupuesto de largo* alcance que se ajuste a nuestras necesidades futuras.

15. Le agradeceré me desglose el total de los siguientes gastos: *acarreo, aduana, embalaje, demora, flete, embarque, remolque, mantenimiento, operación* (corrientes) y *generales.*

UNIT II

ENGLISH AND SPANISH IDIOMS

Part 1   English to Spanish
Part 2   Spanish to English
Part 3   Idiomatic Reinforcements
          Excercises (English to Spanish)

ENGLISH AND SPANISH IDIOMS

Human language is essentially a creative medium adopting new word combinations to express the subtle distinctions in meaning that arise from the changing interactions of group experience. While this dynamic process, reflecting the vitality of colloquial speech, operates in all living languages, each language establishes its own peculiar word formations. Man, therefore, creates new meanings by arranging familiar words in new patterns. These new word combinations are called "idioms".

English is unusually rich in idioms. Their great scope and variety however, are often confusing to non-native English students, and particularly troublesome for beginning translators. One of the reasons for the difficulty involves the intrinsic peculiarities of idioms. They can rarely be modified in syntaxis (word order), nor be altered or substituted by synonyms (similar of like words) without destroying the intended meaning. Moreover, the literal translation of an idiomatic expression defies logic since the specific meaning cannot be derived from combining the meaning of each word or element which constitutes the idiom. Consider, for example, "Pulling my leg" (tomar el pelo).

Students learning English have little option, therefore, but to depend on memory to learn idioms, and on continuous practice, to use them correctly. Obviously, non-native English students or beginning translators cannot be expected to handle (manage) the full range of idiomatic forms which sometimes take a lifetime to master. While translations from Spanish to English can, of course, be rendered without recourse to idioms, an adequate command of the most commonly used idioms is indispensable to capture the conversational, informal style so pervasive in contemporary business writing.

To improve your knowledge of idioms, the following guidelines are useful:

a). Do not depend on the dictionary alone to determine the precise meaning of idioms. Remember, application of the idiom has much to do with the context in which it is used.

b). Talk with native English speakers and observe what idioms they use and how they use them.

33

c). Develop the habit of reading widely in the area of contemporary literature (literaty works, magazines and newspapers in English). This will keep you in touch with current idiomatic usage and change.

The selective group of idioms that follow have been chosen with your particular career needs and professional interests in mind. They serve only as an introduction to the study of English idioms. In Part 1, various definitions of selected English idioms in Spanish have been included to facilitate also the translation material in Part 3.

In Part 2, definitions of selected Spanish idioms applicable to business situations are offered to help you gain further proficiency.

PART 1

ENGLISH TO SPANISH

The following idiomatic expressions will enrich your vocabulary. Translate the sentence carefully and notice the difference between the idiom in English and its translation. Notice also that some of these idiomatic expressions have more than one translation. Choose the one which best fits the context.

1. all along   **desde el principio,**
             en todo momento, todo el tiempo

We knew *all along* that he would be chosen to fill the vacancy.

2. answer the purpose   **convenir, llenar los requisitos, ser**
             adecuado, resolver la cuestión

This assembly room does not *answer our purpose.*

3. apply for a position   **solicitar una colocación**

The plumbers have *applied for the* vacant *positions.*

4. at hand   **a mano**

What information do you have *at hand?* (on hand)

5. better of   **en mejor posición**

We have only three subjects now; therefore we are *better off.*

6. beyond control   **fuera de control, incontrolable**

The fire was *beyond control.*

7. beyond my power   **fuera de mi alcance**

It is *beyond my power* to promote you now because our funds are depleted.

8. beyond dispute   **incontestable, irrefutable**

Her honesty is *beyond dispute.* (beyond doubt)

9. beyond doubt   **fuera de toda duda, indudable**

The truth of the statement is *beyond doubt.*

10. beyond comprehension   **incomprensible, inconcebible**

Her unpleasant attitude is *beyond comprehension.*

11. book an order   **tomar o anotar un pedido para despacho**

The salesman booked our orders for paint and brushes.

12. book a room   **reservar una habitación**

Didn't the tourists *book rooms* in advance?

13. bring about   **efectuar, resultar en, causar, originar**

Her tardiness will *bring about* problems in the near future.

14. call a meeting   **convocar una sesión o una reunión**

Has the student Council *called a meeting* for tomorrow?

15. call for   **preguntar por, pedir, reclamar, procurar, requerir, merecer**

Call for the information we need, please. This situation does not *call for* reprisals.

16. call off   **suspender, cancelar (una reunión, boda, etc.)**

The wedding is *called off* because of serious illness in the family.

17. call on   **visitar a, solicitar**

Call on your best customers during our promotion week.

18. cut in   **interrumpir (la conversación)**

The operator *cut in* when we were talking, so we have to try again to get the information.

19. cut off   **cortar, suspender (servicio)**

The Telephone Company will *cut off* the service if you are in arrears.

20. deals with a problem   **se relaciona con un problema**

His late telephone call *deals with* a serious problem.

21. dispense with   **hacer caso omiso de, renunciar a, pasar sin, prescindir de**

Dispense with the instructions for the time being.

22. dispose of   **vender, deshacerse de, salir de**

Dispose of this material by Monday.

23 do away with   **eliminar, acabar con, suprimir**

The new working schedule will help *to do away with* absences.

36

24. do one's best   **hacer lo mejor posible**

We can't do our best if we are tired.

25. do without   **prescindir de, pasar sin**

Can you *do without* those tools? We don't have them in stock.

26. draw up   **redactar, preparar**

Who has *drawn up* this contract? I don't uderstand the terms.

27. face a situation   **afrontar una situación**

Despite their setbacks, the partnership *faced* the difficult *situation immediately.*   *Saber a que atenerse*

28. figure out   **entender, descifrar, resolver**

Those statistics are so complicated, I can't *figure* them *out.* I can't *figure out* his behavior.

29. file an application   **presentar o enviar una solicitud**

The prospective graduates *have filed applications* in different hotels.

30. get in touch with   **comunicarse con, ponerse en contacto con**

Get in touch with the union leaders and instruct them that they should not *go back on their word.*

31. give out   **emitir, divulgar, distribuir**

Give out these directions to the trainees.
Who *gave out* the information? How did it *leak* out?

32. give up   **renunciar a, entregar, darse por vencido, rendirse, ceder**

When the police surrounded the fugitive, he *gave up.*

33. go back on one's word   **faltar a la palabra dada, retractarse**

Even though they promised to contribute to the fund, they *went back on their word.*

34. go through   **examinar o revisar detenidamente**

Go *through* the report carefully; let me have your decision next week.

35. go through with   **realizar, llevar a cabo**

Go through with the project; you should *live up to your promise.*

36. go without   **pasar sin, arreglárselas sin**

The poor can't *go without* certain staples.

37. go wrong   **salir mal, fracasar**

Everything *went wrong* yesterday because the electricity went off.

38. keep an appointment   **cumplir un compromiso**

Though he was ill, he *kept his appointment* and *made the best of the situation.*

39. keep a record   **llevar un registro**

Keep a record of all those clients who meet their obligations on time.

40. keep up   **mantener, conservar, continuar**

Keep up your enthusiasm and you will succeed.

41. keep one's word   **cumplir con la palabra dada**

The general manager *kept his word* to promote the assistant comptroller.

42. keep up appearances   ¹guardar las apariencias. ²**salvar las apariencias**

To *keep up appearances,* they have mortgaged their home.

**43. live up to someone's expecta-   hacer lo que se espera de uno
tions**

In spite of the shortage of raw materials, we shall *live up to your expectations.*

44. live up to one's promise   **cumplir lo prometido**

The workers *didn't live up to their promise;* some didn't honor the picket line.

45. live within one's income   **vivir de acuerdo al ingreso de uno**

Nowadays it is hard for the average middle class to *live within its income.*

46. look after   **cuidar de, atender a**

Please *look after* my home while I am away.

47. look back   **reflexionar, meditar**

Look back and realize that we have used these tactics before.

48. look for   **buscar, inquirir**

Make up your mind and *look for* a job because we need the money.

49. look forward to   **anticipar (o esperar con agrado o placer)**

The tourist *looks forward to* enjoying the Puerto Rican beaches.

50. look into   **examinar, investigar, averiguar**

The real estate broker will look into the matter before making a decision.

51. look through   **inspeccionar, examinar, registrar, ojear (un libro)**

After the bomb explosion, the police *looked carefully through* the building.

52. make amends   desagraviar, compensar, enmendar

At the meeting, the maintenance crew made a fool of Mr. Rivera. Now they are trying to *make amends.*

53. make both ends meet   ~~pasar con lo que se tiene~~

People in economic difficulties have to do their best to *make both ends meet.*

54. make a fool of   engañar, embaucar, poner en ridículo *hacerse el loco*

He is *making a fool of* himself by his silly comments.

55. make out   descifrar, entender, deducir, imaginar, preparar, llenar (un cheque)

Make me *out* a check for a hundred dollars to pay for theater tickets.

56. make sure   asegurarse de, cerciorarse de

Make sure the heads of department get invitations. *aprovechas la situación*

57. make the best of a situation   soportar, resignarse a la situación

The employees will not be getting the raise; they will just have to *make the best of it.*

sacarle partido a

58. make the most of   sacar (el mayor o mejor) partido posible

The director liked the new trainees, and they *made the most of it.*

59. make up for   compensar por, resarcir

The messenger *made up for* lost time by working extra hours.

60. make up one's mind   decidir, determinar

The Board of Directors will have to *make up their minds* soon or we will lose the bid.

61. make up   hacer las paces (reconciliarse)

After two years of bitter argument the heirs finally *made up.*

62. meet a need   llenar o responder a una necesidad

We are positive that our freezers will *meet the needs* of your meat-importing business.

63. meet an obligation   honrar, pagar, saldar una obligación o deuda

Keep a high credit rating by *meeting your obligation* on time.

64. meet the expenses   hacer frente a los gastos

In order to *meet expenses,* we must collect these overdue debts.

39

65. meet the competition   **hacer frente a la competencia**

The real estate broker, by keeping expenses down, *met the competition* sucessfully.

66. name after   **darle el nombre de** *(ok 2)* *(llamar)*

The union *named* its building *after* Santiago Iglesias. Thus, they kept their promise.

67. obliged to a person (to be)   **estar agradecido a una persona por un favor, obsequio o atención**

I am *obliged to* the Personnel Director for his kindness and understanding.

68. off hand   **de improviso, de momento**

Off hand, I am unable to tell you the products we have undersold.

69. on guard   **en guardia, alerta**

We must be *on guard* when we name the tellers' committee.

70. on no account   **bajo ningún concepto, por ningún motivo**

On no account can you dispose of those funds.

71. on the go   **en movimiento, en actividad constante, activo**

Kissinger was a diplomat *on the go*.

72. on the grounds of   **apoyado en, basado en**

The contractor filed a claim against his client on the *grounds of breach of contract*.

73. on the spur of the moment   **de momento, impulsivamente, sin pensarlo**

He didn't intend to offend you. He made his remarks *on the spur of the moment*.

74. on the way   **de camino, en camino**

I took for granted that the merchandise was *on the way*.

75. out of favor   **en desgracia, (que ya no es el preferido)**

Those who voted against the bill are now *out of favor*.

76. present with   **obsequiar, regalar una cosa a alguien.**

The committee presented the athlete with a medal.

77. put an end to   **acabar con, poner fin a, esmerarse en algo, esforzarse**

The manager took pains to *put an end to* the unpleasant situation.

78. put away guardar, apartar, retirar

The clerk *put away* the perishable articles.

79. put down suprimir, sofocar, apuntar

The dictator *put down* the revolution but the rebels fled the country.

80. put off posponer, aplazar

Put off the meeting until we settle the agenda.

81. put one's foot down ser firme, tomar una resolución

The production manager *put his foot down* because the workers were late.

82. put one's best foot forward esmerarse en hacer lo mejor posible

The new director *put his foot forward.*

83. put on ponerse, encender (la luz) poner encima, disimular, fingir, engañar ganar peso

She has *put on* a lot of weight recently.
Put on the light before you go down the stairs.
The brokers *put on* their best suits for the occasion.
The brokers *put on* their best manners at the reception.
Everybody realized that his affability was a big *put on.*

84. put out apagar (la luz), despedir, irritar, sacar

Put out the intruders who are disturbing the speakers.
The professor was *put out* because there were many students making noise.
Put out as many lights as you can before leaving the house.

85. put up with tolerar, conformarse con, resignarse

The stevedores' strike forced many people to *put up with* what they had.
We can't *put up with* this inconvenience much longer.

86. run for a position ser candidato a un puesto

Who is *running for* mayor of San Juan?

87. run into a person encontrarse con una persona (por casualidad

The student who was absent from the test was very embarrassed when the professor *ran into* him at the movies.

88. take advantage of aprovechar, valerse de, embaucar
to be on one's toes estar alerta

If you are on your toes, you will be able to *take advantage of* the situation.

89. take after   **parecerse a (físico), seguir el ejemplo de**

Mr. Sosa' attitude shows he *takes after* his predecessor.

90. take back   **retractar, desdecir, devolver**

Take back your remarks or I will be forced to file charges against you.

91. take down   **apuntar, descolgar, desmontar una máquina**

The painter *took down* all the pictures that were on the wall.
We must *take* the machine *down* in order to repair it.

92. take for granted   **dar por sentado, no dar importancia a algo**

The foreman *takes for granted* he will get a raise in salary.

93. take into consideration   **tomar en consideración**

Management hasn't *taken into consideration* some of the data we submitted.

94. take off   **quitar(se) la ropa, separar, ponerse en camino, despegar (un avión)**

The plane couldn't *take off* because of bad weather.
Take off your wet clothes or you will catch a cold.

95. take stock   **hacer inventario**

Take stock of our supplies before the truck driver takes off.

96. take pains   **esmerarse en algo, esforzarse**

The auditor *took pains* to verify all the accounts.

97. take place   **tener efecto, celebrarse**

The meeting will *take place* next Monday at the briefing room.

98. tamper with   **manosear, tratar de forzar una cerradura, falsificar un documento corromper**

Don't *tamper with* this machine because it is very complex.
The thief *tampered with* the lock but he couldn't break into the house.

99. tie in with   **concordar con**

The creditor's remarks *tie in with* what the bank official said.

100. tie up (v)   **impedir, obstruir, restringir, dentro de límites, se relaciona con, estar ocupado**

The telephone lines are always *tied up* during Christmas.
The construction of the new overpass *tied up* traffic for six months.
The time certificates of deposit *tie up* people's money for a speci-
fied period.

tie up (n)   **obstrucción en el tránsito**

During heavy rains one can expect a lot of traffic *tie ups*.

PART 2

SPANISH TO ENGLISH

The Spanish language tends to maintain formal modes of expression as standard for communicating in business and other related fields. Nevertheless, the following selected idiomatic forms are common, and a knowledge of their English equivalents will be useful for the business translator.

Translate the sentences that follow and compare your translation with the Spanish original.

1. acabar (con)   **to put an end to, to exhaust, to use up**

Debido a la contínua alza en los costos, nos vemos obligados a *acabar con* la compra de material innecesario de oficina.

2. acabar (por)   **to end up by, finish by, finally**

Después de dilucidar la negociación colectiva *acabaron por* integrar los obreros que habían despedido anteriormente.

3. a cabalidad (a carta cabal)   **thoroughly, completely, in every respect**

La eficiencia de la operación no dejó ninguna duda de que el nuevo gerente conocía sus funciones *a cabalidad.*

4. acreedor a   **deserving of**

El jefe de personal no consideraba al ayudante administrativo *acreedor a* un ascenso inmediato.

5. a estas alturas   **at this advanced stage, at this point, now**

A estas alturas, después de haber invertido tanto dinero en la manufactura del producto, no podemos cambiar el diseño sin incurrir en enormes pérdidas ecónomicas.

6. a partir de (hoy)   **beginning (today)**

A partir de hoy entrarán en vigor las nuevas regulaciones sobre el control de precios.

7. caber la posibilidad   **to be possible**

Cabe la posibilidad de que los empleados se vayan a la huelga en los próximos días.

8. darse cuenta (caer en cuenta)   **to realize; to understand**

No nos dimos cuenta de las implicaciones de su ponencia hasta después de leer el informe completo.

9. dar abasto   **to be adequate, sufficient**
(no dar abasto)   **(to have more than one can handle or manage)**

Una sola secretaria *no da abasto* para escribir a maquinilla todos estos contratos que deben someterse mañana.

10. dar aviso   **to notify, warn**

Al cliente moroso se le *avisó* de que debía enviar su remesa dentro de cinco días.

11. darse de baja   **to drop out (as a member)**

Los estudiantes de la Asociación se *dieron de baja* del seminario auspiciado por la Comisión Industrial.

12. dar crédito   **to believe**

Los consumidores *no dieron crédito* a lo que el Departamento de Asuntos del Consumidor informó sobre los efectos dañinos del detergente.

13. dar muestras de   **to appear to**

Los nuevos cajeros del banco *dan muestras de* ser excelentes oficiales.

14. dar lugar a   **to give rise to**

La fuerte competencia entre las aerolíneas *ha dado lugar* a una baja en las tarifas.

15. de confianza   **of trust**

Muchos de los empleados del gobierno ocupan puestos *de confianza.*

16. dejar margen *de ganancia*   **to bring in more money**

Las ventas realizadas entre los meses de enero a febrero del presente año *han dejado un margen de ganancia* más elevado que las del mismo período del año pasado.

17. desempeñar el puesto de   **to act as**

Por un año, el director de mercadeo *desempeñó el puesto de* presidente interino de la firma.

18. dirigir la palabra   **to address, speak**

El vice presidente pidió a su ayudante que le *dirigiese la palabra a la asamblea.*

19. en calidad de   **in the capacity of, as**

Me dirijo a ustedes *en calidad de* representante de las compañías exportadoras de vino español.

20. estar ajeno a   **to be ignorant of, to be unaware of**

Los accionistas *estaban ajenos a* la precaria situación financiera de la empresa.

21. estar al corriente   **to know about, to be informed**
(al tanto)   **about**

El director ya *está al corriente* (al tanto) de todo.

22. estar en juego   **to be at stake**

La reputación de la directiva *está en juego* con la grave crisis económica por la que atraviesa la corporación.

23. extrañarse de   **to be surprised at**

Todo el mundo *se extrañó de* la rápida penetración del producto en el mercado sin haber tenido la adecuada promoción.

24. formar parte de   **to be part of, to be a member of**

Nuestros productos *forman parte de* los seleccionados para la Feria Internacional.

25. haber cabida   **to have room for, space for**

No hay cabida para las quinientas resmas de papel que acaban de llegar.

26. hacer falta   **to be necessary, needed, missing**

Hace falta que los operadores de teléfono trabajen más eficientemente.

27. hacer partícipe de   **to know about, to tell, inform**
       communicate

Le queremos *hacer partícipe* de la gran venta de ropa formal que comienza el próximo lunes.

28. llevar años con (en)   **to spend years with, to be years with**

El señor jubilado *llevaba treinta años en* el negocio de bienes raíces.

29. hasta nuevo aviso   **until further notice**

La tasa de interés actual se mantendrá al mismo nivel *hasta nuevo aviso.*

30. merecer (valer) la pena — **to be worthwhile**

El anteproyecto de ley *merece la pena* de revisarse en vista de los cambios sugeridos por el departamento de protección al consumidor.

31. pasar por alto — **to overlook, disregard**

Al escribir el informe de nuevo, no debe *pasar por alto* las recomendaciones presentadas por el contador.

32. poner (algo/alguien) a prueba — **to put (something/someone) to the test**

Se ha decidido *poner a prueba* en el mercado un producto plástico experimental.
Se *pusieron a prueba* por un año los nuevos empleados del gobierno.

33. poner de manifiesto — **to show, display, to make public**

El editorial del periódico ha *puesto de manifiesto* el peligro de la inflación desenfrenada.

34. poner en claro (quedar claro) — **to clear up (to be obvious)**

Es imperativo *poner en claro* la directiva financiera que debemos seguir.
Nuestra posición debe *quedar clara* en el convenio colectivo con la unión.

35. saber a qué atenerse — **to know what to expect**

Cuando vayamos a la reunión, debemos estar bien informados para *saber a qué atenernos.*

36. tomar (tener) en cuenta — **to take into consideration, to bear in mind**

Antes de aumentar los precios súbitamente, hay que *tomar en cuenta* la demanda que tiene el producto en el mercado.

37. tenerle al corriente (a alguien) — **to keep (one) posted on, informed about**

El Secretario del Trabajo solicitó al director de la compañía que *le tuviera al corriente* de las negociaciones.

38. tener constancia de — **to have proof of**

El jefe de suministros *tiene constancia* de que la mercancía ha sido confiscada.

39. traer a colación   **to mention, to bring up,**
                                        to raise a question

En la reunión, un miembro del comité *trajó a colación* asuntos ajenos a la agenda.

40. venir al caso (no venir al caso) to be relevant (to be irrelevant)

Esos pormenores no *vienen al caso.*

PART 3

IDIOMATIC REINFORCEMENT EXERCISES
ENGLISH TO SPANISH

The following sentences contain idiomatic expressions you have studied in this unit. In translating them, remember that context is all important to convey the precise meaning and application of the idioms selected.

1. *I look forward* to receiving the data I have requested; otherwise, when we meet, the company spokesmen will take advantage of our lack of information on the subject.

2. *Keep up* your enthusiasm; the response has been *beyond* our *wildest expectations.*

3. He is a resourceful man. This, he proved *beyond doubt* by the way he *put up* with Mr. Rivera's impolite and critical attitude.

4. The *maintenance crew* has been *on the go* since the time we uncovered the full facts about the case.

5. We rent a summer house that we are sure *lives up to your expectations.*

6. *On no account* should you fail to keep your appointment with the broker.

7. Though the young doctor is well off, he is careful with his money; he *takes after* his father in that respect.

8. *On the spur of the moment,* I was unable to describe to the police the man whom I saw *tampering with* the lock.

9. The police *looked through* the house but there was no trace of the robbers.

10. The merchandise you ordered for your summer sale is now *on the way.*

11. *To make up* for our delay, we are sending you complimentary perfume sets for window display.

12. Since *money is tight,* the building company will have to *make both ends meet.*

13. The foreign politician is trying to *make amends* for his unpleasant remarks about our political status.

14. In spite of all their promises, the heirs did not *name* the yacht *after* their father.

15. The speaker's subject will be: "Economics: A Historical Analysis and a *Look Into* the Future."

16. He is *looking into* ways to provide better service at a reasonable price.

17. We are *looking for* a special part to fit the collation machine.

18. His indifference is only *put on*, since I know he doesn't advocate the plan that *calls for* a ban on supplying arms to Israel.

19. The Board of Directors must take strong measures to *meet the mounting competition*.

20. Today the Coast Guard *called off* the search for the missing boat.

21. The senators advocate (favor) *cutting off* aid to countries that expropiate American property without making adequate compensation.

22. The police refused to *give out* details on how they captured the fugitive. After persistent attempts, we *gave up*.

23. I *look forward to* your doing away with "tardiness" in this division.

24. *Get in touch* with the engineer if the two contracts are *put out* for bids.

25. Please decide what you wish *to dispose of* and what to store for future use.

26. The planners are *doing their best* to go *through with* their far-reaching production system.

27. *Make up your mind* carefully if you are thinking about changing jobs.

28. The tellers *went back on their word* when they gave out the results of the voting without *getting in touch with us* first.

29. Please *make the best of the situation*. If the flight is delayed, we shall *look after* you to the best of our ability.

30. I believe that the company directors will *make the most of the situation* since the contract we *drew up* gave them carte blanche to make any changes.

31. The production supervisor urged us to *put off* any decision until we could study the key questions.

32. *Make sure* the employee can *do without* these order forms because we are putting them away until further notice.

33. The Chamber of Commerce *presented* the salesman of the year *with* a commemorative medal.

34. We were embarrassed when someone cut in on the conversation because the subject we were dealing with *called for* extreme confidentiality.

35. The manager will *call a meeting* to discuss the merits of those who have *applied for* the vacant position.

36. Please *book rooms* for the members coming from the States, since I believe hotel space will be solidly booked for next month.

37. The hearing *took place* at San Juan District Court, and the chief witness for the defense made a fool of himself by his evident contradictions.

38. During the strike, Mr. Rosa tried hard *to keep his word,* but the factors he dealt with were beyond his control.

39. *Keep a record* of all the departments that have *gone without* part-time secretaries for the last two months.

40. I don't have *at hand* the names of the banks you should *call on;* please call me again at five.

41. *Take down* the driver's statements, in order to see if they *tie in* with what I have in my notes.

42. The witness *took back* what he had previously sworn to, so the judge held him in *contempt of court.*

43. Before *filing charges* against management, *take into consideration* the Naviera's strike that caused so many shipping *tie ups.*

44. *I take for granted* that you will *touch upon the subject* at the outset. At these meetings, you have to be *on your toes.*

45. The workers were *put out* because the administration continued with the *layoffs.*

46. You will be *better off* if you *meet your obligations* on time.

47. Many people *live beyond their means.* Some get into debt just to *keep up* appearances.

48. It is *beyond comprehension* why the key persons in the plot *dispensed with* precautions.

49. The hearing that *dealt with* the mismanagement of funds was *called off* because of a lack of quorum.

50. The employee has *filed* a $20,000 damage *suit* against the company.

UNIT III
BUSINESS VOCABULARY ENRICHMENT
(English to Spanish)

BUSINESS VOCABULARY ENRICHMENT
(English to Spanish)

The following sentences will enrich your vocabulary because they contain expressions related to everyday business situations. Technical words from banking, shipping and commercial law are included.

You will need to use your dictionary to translate accurately each sentence. Pay particular attention to the meaning of the terms in italics, and be especially careful in translating the technical expressions.

1. The company is reluctant to *allow an exchange on the purchase* because the customer bought that merchandise three weeks ago.

2. When the bank *foreclosed* the mortgage on the farm, Mr. Scott, a famous lawyer, served as counsel to the farmers' union.

3. The *waybills* show that the company shipped the goods following the *consignee's* instructions.

4. The *defendant* contends that he did not alter the content of the letter of credit. He insists that it is a forgery.

5. The *appraiser* told me that Mr. Rivera had become the principal stockholder of the firm because of a *conveyance* of 10,000 shares from his aunt.

6. Since the repairman is a *conscientious* employee, he is reluctant to *commit* himself to finish the job by the deadline requested.

7. When the accident occured, the *insureds* had unfortunately allowed their policy *to lapse* because they had discountinued paying the *premium.*

8. After a long litigation, the *plaintiff* wanted to settle his claim.

9. The company spokesman was very *cautious* about *disclosing* information concerning the client's *breach of contract.*

10. Airlines are forced to comply with *stringent* security measures to protect their passengers.

11. The judge *admonished* the *inmates* who destroyed prison property as a protest against the *crowded* conditions.

12. Our company pride *stems* from the fact that we have never *defaulted* on our payments.

13. The *counterfeits* were made so perfectly that it was impossible to distinguish at first sight which was the false one.

14. The prisoner was *released on parole* because of his *exemplary* behavior.

15. We realize that the *means of conveyance* used in industry affect the *retail price* of an article. But in this case, your *quotations* are *prohibitory* for us.

16. *Labor turnover* and *shortage of skilled workers* have restricted our industrial expansion.

17. We would like to buy the property but *money is tight* and interest rates on loans are high.

18. Many multinational corporations offer attractive *fringe* benefits to employees, such as *life insurance, shares, dividends, bonds* and even academic scholarships for their children.

19. When business is *brisk* there is much more money in circulation than when business is slow. This condition lures consumers to buy goods on the *installment plan* which often leads them *to live beyond their means.*

20. To pay for his *outstanding* debt, the *wholesaler* sent us the following *negotiable instruments endorsed in full:*

    a. *1 mortgage*
    b. *5 stock certificates*
    c. *3 promissory notes*
    d. *10 certified checks.*

21. The heirs are holding *protracted* meetings with the lawyers to discuss the *legacy* because the *testator* has *bequeathed* several chattels to the defendant. Since time is at a *premium,* they will *narrow* their discussions solely to matters that are *germane* to the legal points of view involved.

22. At our office two *correspondence secretaries* provide the typing services for all our *insurance adjusters.*

23. The executive wants to know whether the *return* from his *investment* should be tax *exempt, tax deferred* or taxable.

24. The government loses so much money on *subsidized* homes that it is forced to take over when the owners *default* on their mortgage payments.

25. A corporate secretary:

   a. *keeps the corporate seal,* making sure the company fulfills its legal obligations to stockholders about annual and *interim reports.*

   b. *prepares the proxy material* for the annual meeting, and for the transfer of securities.

   c. maintains records from historical material about the company such as *cancelled dividend checks.*

   d. *keeps minutes* of board meetings.

   e. *prepares the agenda.*

   f. *keeps top executives* and *board directors informed.*

UNIT 4

TRANSITIONAL EXPRESSIONS

Part 1   Functional Categories of Transitions

Part 2   Conjunctions: Coordinate, Subordinate, and Correlative

Part 3   Application of Transitional Expressions (Spanish to English)

TRANSITIONAL EXPRESSIONS

Transitional expressions are words or phrases that serve to establish logical connections between ideas in a sentence , between two or more sentences in a paragraph or between several paragraphs. If the necessary transition is omitted, the reader may lose the trend of thought completely; if the transition is inexact, the reader may be misled. Misused expressions serve only to create confusion.

The following is a list of common transitional words and phrases with examples. They are classified according to their function. Note, however, that some of these transitional terms can be used to indicate more than one relationship between ideas. TRANSLATE THE SENTENCES THAT FOLLOW AND BE SURE YOU GRASP THE PRECISE MEANING AND USE OF EACH TRANSITIONAL EXPRESSION USED.

PART 1

FUNCTIONAL CATEGORIES OF TRANSITIONS

ADDITION

ALSO-ADEMAS...TAMBIEN

A rapid turnover of merchandise is a helpful way to save warehouse costs. *Also*, it allows us to utilize better our limited storage space.

BESIDES-TAMBIEN...ADEMAS

The freight agent is up-to-date on the new export taxation measures; *besides*, he is an expert in handling customs personnel.

FURTHERMORE-ADEMAS

The students cancelled the last two meetings because of repairs to the school auditorium. *Furthermore*, they will probably have to postpone the annual show for the same reason.

IN ADDITION-POR AÑADIDURA...ADEMAS

The general manager approved wholeheartedly of the new marketing strategy; *in addition*, he requested that advertising plans be put into effect immediately.

IN CONCLUSION-EN CONCLUSION...POR ULTIMO

In conclusion, gentlemen, all the questions we have been considering today demonstrate one thing: we have not defined our goals clearly.

FINALLY-FINALMENTE

The personnel officer argued repeatedly that the fundamental obligation was to the institution; *finally*, the dissenting members agreed.

IN THE FIRST PLACE-EN PRIMER LUGAR

Mr. Soto will be a successful diplomat. *In the first place*, he has poise and personality; *in the second place*, he has a broad culture.

65

MOREOVER-ADEMAS

There is great unrest at the factory; *moreover,* the situation is not getting any better because many workers are not interested in listening to reason.

LIKEWISE-ASIMISMO...TAMBIEN

A citizen should be conscious of his rights; *likewise,* he should be conscious of the rights of others and respect them.

CONCESSION

EVEN THOUGH-AUNQUE

Even though the results of the survey could not be guaranteed, we are going to have to make a decision anyway.

ALTHOUGH-AUNQUE

Managers need to be skillful communicators today, *although* this skill is not enough in itself to make a person an effective leader.

AT LEAST-POR LO MENOS

AT ANY RATE-DE TODOS MODOS

The audit evaluation of the client's financial statements was inaccurrate; *at least (at any rate),* that was the opinion of the independent accounting consultant.

STILL-SIN EMBARGO

Banks are generally strict about credit approval; *still,* they sometimes grant loans without adequate collateral.

CONTRAST

BUT-PERO

I side with the students' complaint about the high prices, *but* I take exception to their way of expressing their discontent.

HOWEVER-SIN EMBARGO

The leaders of the association were trying to convince the convention delegates in advance to support the issue. *However,* some of the delegates didn't live up to their promises.

IN CONTRAST-EN CONTRASTE

In Moslem countries, men enjoy excessive privileges; *in contrast,* women's privileges are very limited.

ON THE OTHER HAND-POR OTRA PARTE...EN CAMBIO
ON THE CONTRARY-AL CONTRARIO

Under dictatorships the rights of the citizens are abridged. *On the other hand*, in democracies, some of the citizens abuse many of the rights bestowed on them.

OTHERWISE-DE LO CONTRARIO

You should strive to do your utmost; *otherwise*, you will never be really satisfied.

YET-SIN EMBARGO

The supply on hand is almost used up; *yet*, the purchasing department has done nothing to replenish our stock.

EMPHASIS

OF COURSE-DESDE LUEGO

The general manager agreed wholeheartedly with the production plans. *Of course*, he didn't expect that all phases of the operation would proceed smoothly.

ABOVE ALL-SOBRE TODO, PRINCIPALMENTE

Supervisors must see to it that safety standards are observed throughout the plant. *Above all*, they must regularly check that machine operators follow instructions carefully so as to avoid needless accidents.

INDEED/IN FACT-CLARO, DESDE LUEGO, VERDADERAMENTE

All the technical problems have now been cleared up. *Indeed*, we can finish construction two months before the scheduled deadline.

CERTAINLY/SURELY-CIERTAMENTE, CON CERTEZA

Your $20,000 in government bonds will provide a minimum return on your money. *Certainly*, you might get substantially higher profits by investing in common stocks, but the risk is greater.

EXCLUSION

NEITHER...NOR-NI...NI

Neither the marketing specialist *nor* the financial consultant recommended distribution of the new product before the survey was definitely concluded.

ALL BUT/ALL EXCEPT/TODOS EXCEPTO

When the sales proposals were finally submitted to the general manager, *all but* one were approved.

BUT NOT-PERO NO

Our office receives orders from salesmen *but not* from the general public.

NOT THAT-NO ES QUE

I am unable to accept the commission offered to me last week. *Not that* I feel incapable of successfully discharging the responsibilities; but simply because I will be abroad.

EXPLANATION

FOR EXAMPLE/FOR INSTANCE-POR EJEMPLO

The investigators had to put up with many inconveniences; *for example,* in many offices the staff was not cooperative.

IN PARTICULAR-EN PARTICULAR

We had a pleasant trip to the Scandinavian countries. *In particular,* we enjoyed Norway with its fjords and its midnight sun.

THAT IS-ESTO ES

The new manager is violating established organizational policies; *that is* ,he is overturning the decisions approved by the Board of Directors last year.

SPECIFICALLY-ESPECIFICAMENTE

Many factors are contributing to the inflationary trends in Western countries; *specifically,* the dependence on foreign oil.

PLACE

BEYOND-MAS ALLA...FUERA DE

We believe we have done our best; *beyond that, there is nothing else we can do.*

NEARBY-CERCA...ALLI CERCA...AL LADO

The police found the dead body lying in a ditch; nearby, they found all the victim's belongings.

BESIDE-AL LADO

The plant is on the right-hand side of the road; *beside* it you will see the new industrial park.

PURPOSE

FOR THIS PURPOSE-AL EFECTO...A ESTOS EFECTOS

The president is trying to shorten the meetings. *For this purpose*, he advised us to get in touch with each other to discuss the controversial points and to resolve obvious differences beforehand.

FOR THIS REASON-POR ESTA RAZON

Two laborers died when the scaffolds they were standing on collapsed; *for this reason*, I am going to insist on hiring a safety engineer for our project.

TO THIS END-A ESTE FIN...CON ESTE PROPOSITO

They are attempting every means at their disposal to hamper our activities. *To this end*, they are inciting riots, distributing handbills and broadcasting sensationalist programs.

WITH THIS IN MIND-CON ESTO EN MENTE

The committee believe that the curriculum should serve the students' needs. *With this in mind*, they consulted experts in order to work out new approaches to teaching.

RESULT

AS A RESULT-COMO RESULTADO

Labor shortage, labor turnover, and absenteeism are plaguing our corporation. *As a result*, we have been unable to achieve maximum output as we had expected.

CONSEQUENTLY-POR CONSIGUIENTE...COMO CONSECUENCIA

Many merchants have been buying foreign products at premium prices; *consequently*, they pass on the extra costs to the consumer.

HENCE-POR LO TANTO

The drunk driver drove at full speed and swerved across the road, thus hitting a pedestrian. *Hence*, he was deprived of his driver's license for a year.

THEREFORE-POR LO TANTO...POR ESO

Our desire is to keep our customers; *therefore*, we are granting you ten days grace to settle your account.

THUS-ASI...PUES

We consulted everybody in the classroom; *thus*, all the students could voice their opinion.

TIME

AFTER A SHORT TIME-AL CABO DE CORTO TIEMPO

Immediately after the accident, the claimant filed his petition with the insurance company. *After a short time,* he received the indemnity.

AFTERWARDS-DESPUES...LUEGO...MAS TARDE

Their promises were far-reaching; *afterwards,* they went back on their word and started tampering with freedom of speech and freedom of press.

AT LAST-POR FIN...FINALMENTE...A LA POSTRE

The company spokesman kept on telling the passengers that the flight was delayed. *At last,* when many were going to cancel their bookings, he announced that the plane was taking off within fifteen minutes.

FORMERLY-ANTERIORMENTE

The growth potential of this firm is excellent just now. *Formerly,* I was doubtful because of its poor management.

IN THE MEANTIME-MIENTRAS TANTO

Prepare a list of the home deliveries schedule for next week. *In the meantime,* I shall make the arrangements to expedite our service and avoid delay.

LATER-DESPUES...LUEGO...MAS TARDE

The president complimented the trainees on their tireless efforts. *Later,* he awarded each a scholarship for advanced studies.

THEN-LUEGO

Study this blueprint carefully; *then,* earmark the weak points and give us your suggestions.

WHEN-CUANDO...AL TIEMPO QUE...TAN PRONTO COMO

When you read about the quality of the jobs our plumbing company does, I am positive you will grant us the contract.

PART 2

CONJUNCTIONS: COORDINATE, SUBORDINATE AND CORRELATIVE

A conjunction is a word used to join together or connect words, phrases, and clauses. Conjunctions determine the relationship between the sentence elements they connect. There are three kinds of conjunctions: coordinate, subordinate and correlative.

The following sentences illustrate some common conjunctions. Translate them and notice the meaning and use of the conjunction in question.

COORDINATE CONJUNCTIONS

These connect words or groups of words that are independent of each other. The following are common examples:

AND - Y

The hotel manager deposited the valuables in the safe *and* gave the guest a receipt.

BUT - PERO...SINO

The defendant actually committed the crime, *but* he was acquitted on the grounds of a technical error.

FOR - PUES

The prisoner was released on parole, *for* he had observed faithfully the rules of the penitentiary.

NOR - NI

Do not reveal information on our prospective training programs, *nor* disclose the names of the would-be-trainees.

OR - O

You may sort the merchandise to be sent to the storeroom, *or* you may continue tallying the accounts.

SUBORDINATE CONJUNCTIONS

A subordinate conjunction relates a clause which has less contextual emphasis to the main clause or to another subordinate clause.

ALTHOUGH - AUNQUE...NO OBSTANTE

Although the guarantee on your stereo components has expired, we shall send you free of charge the parts you requested.

AS - YA QUE...COMO...SEGUN...CONFORME

I shall abstain from voting, *as* I believe Mr. Serra is not adapted for the job.
Oil the motor *as* the instructions specify.

BECAUSE - (PORQUE)...DEBIDO A ...A CAUSA DE

Because of the severe drought, the Water Resources Authority rationed supply.

BEFORE - ANTES

Before you draw up your conclusions, find out the truth about the hearsay you have reported.

IF - SI

If our company planners get advance approval of the site they have chosen, they can maneuver to apply for an appropriation ahead of schedule.

PROVIDED THAT - SIEMPRE QUE...A CONDICION DE QUE...CON TAL QUE

The recipients of government grants are not unworthy, *provided* they manage the funds properly.

SINCE - COMO...DESDE

Since many government funds have been frozen, money for the opening of new schools is at a premium.
I have not seen the former governor *since* the new party came into power.

THAN - QUE

Our competitors are offering the Japanese dinnerware at a price lower *than* the original.
Our products are of a higher quality *than* theirs.

UNLESS - A MENOS QUE...A NO SER QUE

Unless we analyze our new product carefully, we shall be unable to eliminate potential complaints before it reaches the market.

WHEN - CUANDO

When the association holds protracted meetings, the president always tells his secretary to arrange lunch for us.

There are some subordinate conjunctions that are composed of two or three words. These are called phrasal conjunctions. The most commonly used phrasal conjunctions follow.

AS THOUGH - COMO SI

AS IF - COMO SI

At the bidding, the realtor acted *as if* he had a lot of money to dispose of.

EVEN THOUGH - A PESAR DE QUE

Even though we took safety measures, the storm disrupted our telephone service.

IN CASE (THAT) - EN CASO DE QUE

In case you lose the instructions, phone me immediately.

IN ORDER THAT - DE MANERA QUE...A FIN DE QUE

The metal has been treated *in order that* it may resist corrosion under extreme weather conditions.

PROVIDED (THAT) - A CONDICION DE QUE...SIEMPRE QUE

These shirts will give you excellent service, *provided* you follow the instructions on the label.

SO THAT - DE MODO QUE...DE SUERTE QUE

So that you may have the wire-bound containers for the rush season, we are sending them by air cargo.

CORRELATIVE CONJUNCTIONS

These are used in pairs to join sentence elements of equal grammatical importance. They are also used as connectives between subordinate and main clauses. Common correlatives are:

AS...AS - TAN...COMO

As soon as Mr. Silva knew that people alien to the institution took part in the activities, he called a meeting.

ALTHOUGH/STILL - AUNQUE...AUN

Although Juan's grade in the competitive examination was low, *still* he expects to get the certificate.

BOTH/AND - AMBOS...Y...TANTO...COMO

Both the left-wing *and* right-wing groups are morally responsible for the continuing disorders.

EITHER...OR - UNO U OTRO...O...O

Either the labor leader *or* management will have to give in before the crisis reaches a climax.

IF...THEN - SI...ENTONCES

If the product has not lived up to the advertisement, then ask for an exchange on it.

NEITHER...NOR - NI...NI

Neither his accusations *nor* his treats will deter me from defending my point of view.

NOT ONLY...BUT ALSO - NO SOLO...SINO, NO SOLAMENTE...SI NO

Not only did they trample on the rights of the group, *but* they *also* claimed they were attacked.

SO...AS - TAN...COMO

The assistant was *so* kind *as* to help me get the information.

WHETHER...OR - SI...O

The engineer asked us *whether or* not we agreed to pledge the stocks on short notice.

PART 3

APPLICATION OF TRANSITIONAL EXPRESSIONS
(Spanish to English)

1. Un hombre de negocios debe cumplir con sus compromisos a tiempo, además, debe mantener buenas relaciones con el público.

2. Aunque varias escuelas de Estados Unidos estaban renuentes a aceptar la integración, finalmente, muchas han acatado la ley. No obstante, todavía habrá serios disturbios que pondrán en peligro tanto la vida de los alumnos como la de los profesores.

3. Este producto no llena los requisitos federales ni tampoco nuestras necesidades.

4. Hasta este momento el oficial se ha defendido muy bien; además se ha presentado evidencia adicional a su favor. En conclusión, no creo que él renuncie.

5. Conoce tus derechos; asimismo, reconoce y respeta los de los demás.

6. No veo por qué objetan su nombramiento; después de todo, él es la persona idónea para llenar la vacante.

7. Estamos preparando nuestra campaña de promoción. Al mismo tiempo, estamos dando instrucciones a todas las sucursales para que den adiestramiento a sus empleados.

8. El viajero tenía la apariencia de un hombre de negocios serio, sin embargo, según la aduana comprobó, era un contrabandista en drogas.

9. Le aconsejamos que no gastara más de lo que ganaba. Aún asi, no nos hizo caso y es por esta razón que no pudo cumplir su compromiso a tiempo y el banco ejecutó la hipoteca.

10. Conserva el talonario de cheques con la información necesaria. De otro modo, puede que tengas problemas a fin de mes.

11. Me encantó el discurso del presidente, especialmente, cuando dijo que él practica lo que predica.

12. Nos harán concesiones especiales en la reunión. Esto es, nos aprobarán el proyecto, aunque el presupuesto para éste es muy alto.

13. Esperamos demostraciones esta semana. Al efecto, estamos tomando las medidas necesarias para no tèner problemas con los obreros.

14. Los estudiantes publicaron su petición en el periódico. Como resultado, recibieron miles de adhesiones.

15. Ya que el salón de conferencias estará ocupado para esa fecha, por lo menos, deberían prestarnos el salón de adiestramiento.

16. Escribimos al Sr. Sosa que descontinuara el uso de su tarjeta de crédito. Renuentemente, nos la devolvió tres meses después.

17. Por ley, los huelguistas no pueden celebrar mítines ni exhibir cartelones en los terrenos del negocio.

18. A pesar de que el automóvil estaba asegurado, el peatón demandó al conductor por una cantidad adicional.

19. Puedes visitar los países detrás del Bloque Comunista, siempre y cuando no hagas comentarios negativos acerca del régimen.

20. Puedes disfrutar de todos los privilegios siempre y cuando hagas el uso debido de ellos.

21. Tan pronto como levanten la prohibición de envío de medicinas a Cuba, podremos enviar antibióticos a nuestros amigos.

22. Ni uno ni otro grupo cede. Por lo tanto, las negociaciones están estancadas. Esta situación deplorable no sólo afecta a los obreros sino que también a la empresa.

23. Juan y Carlos no desean trabajar horas extra. No obstante debemos pedirle su cooperación por este período ya que estamos cortos de personal.

24. Como el testador no dejó instrucciones claras en su testamento, por el momento, su hijo no puede disfrutar de la herencia, ni el estado puede cobrar los impuestos.

25. Ellos actúan como si tuviesen mucho dinero para invertir en el negocio. Aún asi, tengo mis dudas porque en anteriores ocasiones han estado sólo especulando.

26. Dos miembros se abstuvieron de votar la propuesta, sin embargo, el tesorero luego de haber objetado parte de la moción, votó a su favor.

27. En muchos municipios las facilidades médicas son deplorables, no obstante la necesidad imperiosa que hay de ellas.

28. De modo que pueda estimular a sus trabajadores a producir el máximo, le estamos incluyendo algunos planes diseñados a ese efecto.

29. Presumo que he disipado sus dudas respecto a esta transacción, a no ser que usted tenga otros puntos que desee aclarar.

30. Debido a la explosiva situación existente, preparamos de inmediato planes para casos de contingencia, a menos que usted lo requiera de otro modo.

UNIT 5

AUXILIARY VERBS IN INTERROGATIVE STRUCTURES

Part 1   Syntactical Comparison of English and Spanish Interrogative
          Forms

Part 2   Auxiliary verbs *to do* and *to have*

Part 3   Semantic Function of Modal Auxiliaries in English and Spanish
          Syntax

Part 4   Interrogative Words

Part 5   Use of There + Be as Equivalent of Haber

Part 6   Reinforcement Exercises

79

AUXILIARY VERBS IN INTERROGATIVE STRUCTURES

Since question forms are so fundamental in language learning, their inclusion in a translation course might be viewed by readers as unnecessary. Mastery of the English question form, however, even after years of instruction, eludes many second-language learners. The fact that a significant proportion of students are reluctant to ask questions in English points to a recurring problem in this area. Some reason that their lack of proficiency with the English question form results from vocabulary inadequacies. It is our belief - a belief conformed by experience - that the problem is directly related to a continuing insecurity with the structural forms themselves.

It is not our intention to review systematically all the fundamentals of English interrogative structures in this unit. Our objective is to establish, by way of comparison and contrast, the basic syntactical patterns of questions which incorporate the use of auxiliary verbs, particularly the troublesome *do/have*, and the modals. The semantic comparison of the modal auxiliaries is included because they are so necessary for translating subtlety of meaning. Moreover, a review of common interrogative words is included to facilitate proper syntax and meaning as well as a section on the impersonal use of the verb *to be*. Along with the reinforcement exercises offered in the text, the resourceful teacher will supplement the unit with explanations and exercises (such as compound question forms - in what way/to what degree/contractions of auxiliaries in question forms, etc.) as the particular needs of students dictate.

PART 1

SYNTACTICAL COMPARISON OF ENGLISH AND SPANISH INTERROGATIVE FORMS

Before dealing with the problems of interrogative structures, it is important to review the basic syntactical difference of English and Spanish questions. Observe the following example which demonstrates this fundamental difference:

Spanish question form

¿Había terminado la secretaria el informe ayer antes de que yo llamara?

¿Había la secretaria terminado el informe ayer antes de que yo llamara?

¿La secretaria había terminado el informe ayer antes de que yo llamara? (Intonation in spoken Spanish shows this to be a question)

English Translation

Had the secretary finished the report yesterday before I called?

Notice that Spanish admits a variation in question form, English, on the other hand, establishes a fixed, inflexible word order. In interrogative sentences using the present and past tense of the verb *to be*, the order will always be:

Verb	Subject	Rest of the Sentence
Is	John	an accountant?
Were	you	at the conference?

In all other question forms in English where an auxiliary verb comes into play, the order will always be:

Auxiliary Verb	Subject	Main Verb	Rest of the Sentence
Had	the secretary	finished	the report yesterday before I called?

To visualize this word order study the following examples.

1. The electrician is looking for a job.

    Is the electrician looking for a job?

El electricista está buscando trabajo.
¿Está el electricista buscando trabajo?

2. The manager was itemizing the deductions.
Was the manager itemizing the deductions?

El gerente estaba detallando las deducciones.
¿Estaba el gerente detallando las deducciones?

3. The customer is not withdrawing the complaint.
Isn't the customer withdrawing the complaint?

El cliente no esta retirando su queja.
¿No está el cliente retirando su queja?

4. The company will formulate contingency plans to meet the fuel shortage.
Will the company formulate contingency plans to meet the fuel shortage?

La compañía formulará medidas de contingencia para afrontar la escasez de combustible.
¿Formulará la compañía medidas de contingencia para afrontar la escasez de combustible?

5. The strikers have disclosed that they planned their strike a month ago.
Have the strikers disclosed that they planned their strike a month ago?

Los huelguistas han revelado que ellos planearon su huelga hace un mes. ¿Han revelado los huelguistas que ellos planearon su huelga hace un mes?

6. The mortgagee has not extended the payment deadline. Hasn't the mortgagee extended the payment deadline?

El tenedor de la hipoteca no ha prorrogado la fecha límite de pago.
¿No ha prorrogado el tenedor de la hipoteca la fecha límite de pago?

7. The three men had stolen the jewels from the safe when the police arrived. Had the three men stolen the jewels from the safe when the police arrived?

Los tres hombres habían robado las joyas de la caja de seguridad cuando la policía llegó.
¿Habían robado los tres hombres las joyas de la caja de seguridad cuando la policía llegó?

8. The company spokeswoman had not given us the information on time.
Hadn't the company spokeswoman given us the information on time?

La portavoz de la compañía no nos había dado la información a tiempo.

— ¿No nos había dado la portavoz de la compañía la información a tiempo?

9. The longshoremen have been working all night.
   Have the longshoremen been working all night?

   Los estibadores han estado trabajando toda la noche.
   —¿Han estado los estibadores trabajando toda la noche?

10. Our department has not been selling much French perfume lately.
    Hasn't our department been selling much French perfume lately?

    Nuestro departamento no ha estado vendiendo mucho perfume francés últimamente.
    — ¿No ha estado vendiendo nuestro departamento mucho perfume francés últimamente?

11. The inmates had been acting suspiciously.
    Had the inmates been acting suspiciously?

    Los reclusos habían estado actuando sospechosamente.
    — ¿Habían estado los reclusos actuando sospechosamente?

12. We had not been using disposable containers before.
    Hadn't we been using disposable containers before?

    No habíamos estado usando envases desechables anteriormente.
    — ¿No habíamos estado usando envases desechables anteriormente?

13. The workers shall have unloaded the perishable foodstufs early tomorrow.
    Shall the workers have unloaded the perishable foodstuffs early tomorrow?

    Los trabajadores habrán descargado los comestibles perecederos mañana temprano.
    — ¿Habrán descargado los trabajadores los comestibles perecederos mañana temprano? _awkward_

14. If you were the defendant company, you would act likewise.
    If you were the defendant company, would you act likewise?

    Si usted fuera la compañía demandada, actuaría del mismo modo.
    ¿Si usted fuera la compañía demandada, actuaría del mismo modo?

15. If they had been the tellers, they would have counted the votes in one hour.
    If they had been the tellers, would they have counted the votes in one hour?

    Si ellos hubiesen sido los escrutadores, hubieran contado los votos en una hora.
    ¿Si ellos hubiesen sido los escrutadores, hubieran contado los votos en una hora?

Notice that when the negative (not) is contracted, it is attached to the auxiliary verb; otherwise, it is placed before the main verb.

PART 2

AUXILIARY VERBS *TO DO* **AND** *TO HAVE*

To do is both an action verb (translated in Spanish as *hacer*) as well as an important auxiliary verb in English. As an auxiliary verb it has two particular functions:

1. to give emphasis in declarative sentences. Notice the emphatic function and translation of *do* in the following declarative sentence.

   They do write letters   *Ellos sí escriben cartas*
   every day.   *todos los días.*

2. to formulate questions where the present and simple past tenses of the verb are used (with the exception of the verb *to be*, as we have observed in Part 1). In the following question form, notice the importance of the auxiliary *do:*

   Do they write letters   ¿Escriben ellos cartas
   every day?   todos los días?

   The auxiliary *do* is essential in the English question when the verb is in the present or the past tense. On the other hand, the auxiliary *do* has no function in the Spanish sentence because Spanish does not need this auxiliary to phrase questions.

   There are three forms for the auxiliary: DO, DOES, and DID which are used to indicate differences in person and time.

In the present indicative use DOES before a subjet in the third person singular:

    Does Marie speak Italian?   ¿Habla María italiano?
    Does she go to the   ¿Va ella al teatro?
    theater?
    Does he sell jewelry?   ¿Vende él joyería?
    Does it require a reply?   ¿Requiere eso una cons-
                                  testación?

Notice that when we use DOES, we drop the *s* ending from the verb. Only the auxiliary carries the *s.*

Use **DO** for all other subjects in the present indicative:

Do I qualify?	¿Cualifico?
Do you smoke	¿Fuma usted?
Do they sign the	¿Firman ellos el docu-
document also?	mento también?
Do the plumbers	¿Ganan los plomeros
earn much?	mucho dinero?

Use **DID** as a signal of the past tense for *all* persons:

Did I pass the test?	¿Aprobé el examen?
Did we succeed?	¿Triunfamos?
Did she agree?	¿Estuvo ella de acuerdo?
Did Pedro win the	¿Ganó Pedro el certamen?
contest?	

It is important to notice that in the PRESENT as well as in the PAST tense, whenever you use the auxiliaries DO, DOES, and DID, the verb that follows the subject is in the BASIC or SIMPLE form.

DO, DOES, DID are also used in conversation as a substitute for the verb in elliptical answers to avoid repetition:

Do you like it?	I do.
¿Te gusta?	Sí.
Does John swim?	He doesn't.
¿Nada Juan?	No.
Did they sing?	They did.
¿Cantaron ellos?	Sí.

-Study the examples of the use of the auxiliary *to do* in the diagrammatic pattern below. Notice that the word order follows the general rule of syntax for English question form we reviewed in Part 1.

-In the following sentences, convert the English declarative sentence into English question form.

-Compare the question form in Spanish with your English version.

Sentence	Auxiliary	Subject	Verb	Rest of Sentence
1	Does	this situation	alienate	many voters from the party?
2	Do	the masons	finish	their work today?

1. This situation alienates many voters from the party.

   Esta situación aleja a muchos votantes del partido.
   ¿Aleja esta situación a muchos votantes del partido?

2. The masons finish their work today.

   Los albañiles terminan su trabajo hoy.
   ¿Terminan los albañiles su trabajo hoy?

3. The maintenance supervisor does not agree with our policies.

   El supervisor de mantenimiento no está de acuerdo con nuestras normas.
   ¿No está el supervisor de mantenimiento de acuerdo con nuestras normas?

4. The phone call dealt with the delicate situation that we are facing.

   La llamada telefónica trataba sobre la delicada situación que estamos afrontando.
   ¿Trataba la llamada telefónica sobre la delicada situación que estamos afrontando?

5. The phone call did not deal with the delicate situation we are facing.

   La llamada telefónica no trataba sobre la delicada situación que estamos afrontando.

   ¿No trataba la llamada telefónica sobre la delicada situación que estamos afrontando?

Since the correct use of this auxiliary is so important for clarity in translation, let us underscore what we have already said. The auxiliary *to do* has an essential function in the English question form. While it has no independent meaning in English questions, it does have a function to indicate differences in person (DO/DOES) and in present and past tense (DO, DOES/DID). Since the Spanish language indicates differences in person and time through verbal endings (hablo, hablan, habló, hablaban, etc.), *to do* has no function at all in Spanish. Moreover, as we have seen, Spanish has to employ a modifier to indicate the emphatic function of the auxiliary *to do* in declarative sentences.

TO HAVE, like *TO DO*, is both an active verb and an auxiliary. As an active verb it is translated in Spanish as TENER (just as DO is translated in Spanish as HACER); as an auxiliary it is translated as HABER. Once this distinction is clearly noted, the use of TO HAVE (HABER), should represent little difficulty for the beginning translator. Like TO DO, it does make distinction for the third person singular HAS. It is used in both languages to indicate corresponding time differences between the present perfect and the past perfect tenses; nevertheless, as the examples below show, the auxiliary has identical function and meaning in both English and Spanish.

In the present perfect indicative, use HAS before a subject in the third person singular.

Has she paid her bill?	¿Ha pagado ella su cuenta?
Has he finished already?	¿Ha terminado él ya?
Has the order arrived?	¿Ha llegado el pedido?

Use HAVE for all other subjects in the present perfect indicative.

Have you bought the house?	¿Ha comprado usted la casa?
Have the drivers returned?	¿Han regresado los conductores?

Use HAD for all subjects in the past perfect.

Had she drunk the medicine?	¿Había tomado ella la medicina?
Had they sent her account number?	¿Habían enviado ellos el número de la cuenta de ella?
Had the physician seen the patient?	¿Había visto el doctor al paciente?

Notice the differences in syntax or word order in question form remain the same. All auxiliaries in English, including to have, follow the general rule for question form established in Part 1 of this unit.

PART 3

SEMANTIC FUNCTION OF MODAL AUXILIARIES
IN ENGLISH AND SPANISH SYNTAX

The modal auxiliaries function in the same way as other auxiliary forms. They have, however, important semantic consequences in both declarative and interrogative structures. They are used to convey shades of meaning; that is, they add a particular meaning to the verbs with which they are used. By using these auxiliaries with main verbs, the total meaning of the verb phrase is modified to include such concepts as: permission, ability, necessity, possibility, duty, etc. Look at the examples below:

I *may* (or might) come to see you. (Possibility)
You *may* call her up if you like. (Permission)
You *might* let me know what she decides to do. (Suggestion)
I *can* or *could* tell her the details of the interview. (Ability)
We *must* tell her the details of the interview. (Compulsion, necessity)
He *should* come. (Obligation, duty)
She *would* come. (Volition, likelihood)
She *would* not come. (Unwillingness, determination)

The translated examples that follow illustrate that for your purpose, there is hardly any distinction between English and Spanish modal auxiliaries either in meaning or use.

MAY is generally used to express permission.

May the accountant leave early today? (permission requested)	¿Puede irse el contable (contador) temprano hoy?
Yes, the accountant may leave early today. (permission granted)	Sí, el contable (contador) puede irse temprano hoy.

MAY is also used to express possibility of doing something.

I may go to the theater this weekend.	Puede que vaya al teatro este fin de semana.

MIGHT, however, also expresses possibility: in fact, it is interchangeable with MAY.

She might call up tomorrow.	Puede que ella telefonée mañana.
He might go to the university next year.	Puede que él vaya a la universidad el próximo año.

CAN means PODER (to express ability or potential)

Can you finish early?	¿Puedes terminar temprano?
Can she run a mile?	¿Puede ella correr una milla?

CAN is also used to mean SABER

Can you play the piano?	¿Sabes tocar piano?
Can they teach French?	¿Saben ellos enseñar francés?

COULD is used to express:

-- ability at a previous time

When I was young, I could run fast	Cuando yo era joven, podía correr rápidamente,

-- a polite request

Could you get me a glass of wine?	¿Me podrías traer un vaso de vino?
Could we see you tomorrow?	¿Podríamos verle mañana?

-- a shade of doubt

Could that be true?	¿Podría ser eso verdad?

SHOULD is used to express advisability but not in the sense of an absolute obligation, duty or necessity.

The disabled should get special care.	Los incapacitados deben recibir atención especial.
My supervisor is sick, I should go to see him.	Mi supervisor está enfermo, debo irlo a ver.

It also expresses expectation or probability.

Since my sister left Saturday, she should be here by Monday evening.	Como mi hermana partió el sábado, ella debe estar aquí para el lunes en la noche.
They should graduate by next June.	Ellos deben graduarse para el próximo junio.

WOULD is used to express condition or a softened request.

The lecturer would come if you would ask her.	La conferenciante vendría si tú se lo pidieses.
I would accompany you with pleasure.	Te acompañaría con gusto.
Would you help me?	Me ayudarías?

WOULD can express a customary action in the past.

I would go to the beach on Sundays when I was living in Florida.	Solía ir a la playa los domingos cuando vivía en Florida.

WOULD can express a desire.

I would like to talk to you.	Me gustaría hablar contigo.

WOULD can express a condition when it is used with an *if* clause.

If you had called me up, I would have given you the money.	Si me hubieses llamado, te hubiera dado el dinero.
If I were rich, I would go to Europe in the spring.	Si yo fuera rico iría a Europa en la primavera.

WOULD can express a preference when used in combination with *rather*.

He would rather go to the movies than study.	El preferiría ir al cine en vez de estudiar.

WOULD can express a negative attitude when used with *not*.

I wouldn't go to that restaurant again.	Yo no iría a ese restaurante otra vez.

MUST means DEBER, TENER QUE, SER NECESARIO, SER MENESTER (closer to the absolute sense of obligation.

You must pay your monthly bills.	Usted debe pagar sus cuentas mensuales.

MUST also may be used to imply probability or certainty.

The clerk must have been sick if he didn't finish the work on time.	El oficinista debe haber estado enfermo, si no terminó su trabajo a tiempo.
She must have gone when you arrived.	Ella debe haberse ido cuando tú llegaste.

Notice that in the sense stated above, MUST is used before HAVE and participial form.

OUGHT TO also means DEBER, TENER QUE

Of the modal auxiliaries this is the only one that is always followed by the preposition *to*.

You ought to send her the cable on Monday.	Debes (debieras) enviarle el cable el lunes.
I ought to answer this letter within three days.	Tengo que contestar esta carta dentro de tres días.

If the instructor feels that further practice in using the modal auxiliaries is necessary, the following suggestions might be helpful.

1. The material of the units already covered could be profitably adapted to include the modal either in the declarative or interrogative forms. Since the students are already familiar with the vocabulary of this material the adaptation should be relatively easy for them.

2. To practice the variety of modal forms students could write original sentences either in Spanish or English using the wording of the material already studied.

3. Students could be asked to bring to class examples of the use of modal auxiliaries as observed in local newspapers or magazines, for example.

PART 4
INTERROGATIVE WORDS

1. A list of interrogative words and their Spanish equivalent follow for your review. These words are used in questions that require an answer that is more specific than a simple Yes or No. The Wh word represents the type of information wanted.

What	¿qué?
What kind of?	¿qué clase de?
What time?	¿a qué hora?
Which	¿cuál?
When	¿cuándo?
Where	¿dónde?
Who	¿quién?
Whom	¿(a) (para) quién?
Whose	¿de quién?
Why	¿por qué?
How	¿cómo?
How far	¿a qué distancia?
How many	¿cuánto, cuánta, cuántas?
How long	¿cuánto mide (de largo, ancho)?
How often	¿con qué frecuencia?

Here you are given interrogative statement in English that contain the expressions given above. Your assignment is *to convert them to Spanish and supply the answer in English to each question.*

Ex. When does the invoice fall due?   ¿Cuándo vence el pagaré?
    Short answer: On the 27th of this month
    Complete answer: The invoice falls due on the 27th of this month.

1. *What* has the marketing manager told you?
2. *What* kind of computer have they acquired?
3. *What* does the new engineer do during his time off?
4. *When* did the trade-union present their cogent letter?
5. *Where* do they keep the imprinted envelopes?
6. *Where* did you meet a member of the Board?
7. *Which* students have been getting high grades?

9. *Who* was reviewing the itemized invoice?
10. *Who* are going to the convention?
11. *Whose* names will appear on the list?
12. *Why* is the General Supervisor working in the Data Processing Department?
13. *How* does the bank handle the stale checks?
14. *How many* members of the Board of Directors are reluctant to sign the petition?
15. *How far* did the bus take you?
16. *How long* will the appraisal of the property take?
17. *How much* money did the defendant embezzle?
18. *How often* does the purchasing power of the dollar go up?
19. *Which brand* of cigarettes is your favorite?
20. *What time* will be convenient for you, if we meet tomorrow?

In this part you are given the interrogative statements containing question words in Spanish. Your assignment is to translate these statements into English.

1. ¿Quiénes votaron por poder?
2. ¿Quién es el acusado de desfalco?
3. ¿Cuándo vencía la hipoteca?
4. ¿Por qué se han mudado los inquilinos?
5. ¿Cómo podríamos monopolizar el mercado?
6. ¿Dónde está la copia del testamento?
7. ¿Qué argumento convincente ha presentado el arquitecto en la vista?
8. ¿Cuáles revistas prefieres?
9. ¿Cuán a menudo tiene esa firma problemas obrero patronales serios?
10. ¿Cuántas veces has cambiado de empleo?
11. ¿Cuántos envases plásticos tenemos?
12. ¿De quién son estas medicinas?
13. ¿Cuánto costaban esos impermeables el año pasado?
14. ¿Qué hora te conviene más para celebrar la reunión?
15. ¿Por cuánto tiempo te quedarías con nosotros?
16. ¿Cuál prefieres?
17. ¿A dónde viajarás el próximo verano?
18. ¿De quiénes son estos paquetes?
19. ¿Para quién es este escritorio?
20. ¿A qué distancia está la estación de gasolina?
21. ¿A quién se refirieron ellos?
22. ¿Cuántos pies de largo mide tu terraza?
23. ¿Cuántos pies de ancho mide tu terraza?
24. ¿Cuántos pies de alto tiene la cerca?
25. Eres muy alto. ¿Cuánto mides?

PART 5
USE OF THERE + BE AS EQUIVALENT OF HABER

The translation of the expletive THERE causes trouble to Spanish-Speaking students because THERE has no translation in Spanish. It is important to learn that the expression HABER is expressed in English with the form BE (without TO) and with the form THERE in the position of the subject.

Negative statements are formed by placing NOT after the verbs in the simple tenses; and by placing NOT after the auxiliary in the compound tenses.

There is not a cloud in sight.	No hay ni una nube a la vista.
There will not be refreshments.	No habrá refrescos.

Interrogative statements place THERE in the second position.

Is there anybody here?	¿Hay alguien aquí?

The examples given below are intended to clarify doubts and to highlight differences existing between the Spanish and the English equivalent.

CONJUGATION

1. *Present*

   Hay mucho que hacer en nuestra compañía.
   There is much to be done in our company.
   Hay dos trabajadores diestros ausentes en esta mañana.
   There are two skilled workmen absent this morning.

2. *Present Perfect*

   Ha habido aumento en la adicción a drogas.
   There has been an increase in drug addiction.   *Han habido*

   Ha habido varios cambios en la agenda.
   There have been various changes in the agenda.

97

3. *Past*

Hubo un accidente en el aeropuerto.
There was an accident at the airport.

Había muchos extranjeros en la actividad.
There were many foreigners in the activity.

4. *Past Perf.*

Había habido discrepancias entre los dos acusados.
There had been discrepancies between the two defendants.

5. *Future*

Habrá una exhibición de microcomputadoras en el salón 412.
There will be a display of microcomputers in room 412.

6. *Future Perf.*

Cuando regreses, *habrá habido* muchos cambios.
Upon your return, *there will have been* many adjustments.

7. *Conditional*

Habría desasosiego en el grupo, si estuviésemos descontentos.
There would be unrest in the group, if we were dissatisfied.

8. *Conditional Perf.*

Habría habido un aumento de salario, si hubiésemos hecho las ventas que esperábamos.
There would have been a salary increase, if we had made the sales we expected.

Translate the following sentences and pay close attention to the position of the verb in the sentence.

1. ¿Hay muchos condominios sin vender?
2. ¿No había muchos estudiantes en el seminario?
3. ¿Hubo muchas alzas y bajas en el mercado el año pasado?
4. ¿No ha habido protesta debido a estas instrucciones?
5. ¿Había habido controversias anteriormente?
6. ¿No habrá oposición a nuestro horario?
7. ¿Habrá habido noticias sobre los ascensos?
8. ¿Hay escasez de productos de primera necesidad?
9. ¿No hay cinco empleados que puedan trabajar horas extra?
10. ¿Ha habido cambios drásticos en el programa de adiestramiento?
11. ¿Hubo una persona que se abstuvo de votar?
12. ¿No habrá un proyecto especial para aquellos estudiantes que obtuvieron notas bajas en el examen?
13 ¿Habría habido fondos para comprar el equipo, si hubiésemos vendido las acciones?
14. ¿Había promesa de entregar la nevera ya reparada dentro de diez días?
15. ¿No habría inconvenientes si trabajamos una hora extra?

PART 6

REINFORCEMENT EXERCISES

A. Here you are given the situation. Your assignment is to *formulate the question from the statement in English.*

    Ex. Ask the merchant if he has replenished the stock.
        Have you prepared your resumé?

    1. Ask your friend if she has read the headlines.
    2. Ask the clerk if the engineer has the part for the computer.
    3. Ask your friend the meaning of the expressions "vindictive", "jeopardy".
    4. Ask your friend the reason for not calling you up.
    5. Ask your professor the time the outline has to be handed in.
    6. Ask the secretary of the committee the times they have withheld information from the press.
    7. Ask the accountant if Mr. Suárez had to pay interest on the loan due.
    8. Ask the secretary if she wanted to attend the seminar.
    9. Ask the mechanic if he listens to the morning news.
   10. A friend of yours will be appointed delegate to the convention.
       You don't know who the person will be. Ask your boss.

B. Here you are given the situation. Your assignment is *to formulate the question in English from the statement in Spanish.*

    Ex. Pregunte al guardia de seguridad   Have you prepared your
        Si ha preparado su resumé.   resumé?

Pregunte:

    1. a María si ha leído el último boletín del tiempo.
    2. a la secretaria si el ingeniero tiene la pieza para la máquina electrónica.
    3. al presidente de la compañía si ya ellos habían vendido la producción total cuando recibieron el cable.

4. a la recepcionista si ella deseaba tomar un día libre.
5. a la profesora cuándo tenemos que entregar el informe.
6. al tesorero de la compañía las veces que han negado información a la prensa.
7. a los estudiantes si ellos van a la fiesta mañana.
8. a Juan si el Sr. Medina tenía que pagar interés alto sobre la hipoteca.
9. a su hermano si el iría con usted a Nueva York.
10. a su secretaria cuándo el asistente del arquitecto renunciará su puesto.
11. a su amigo cuáles son los puntos sobresalientes de la querella.
12. a la secretaria por qué el recaudador huyó con el dinero.
13. al ingeniero si la escasez de mano de obra y los cambios de personal han afectado a los fabricantes.
14. al comerciante si el problema había sido resuelto.
15. a Juan si el secretario tiene tiempo esta tarde para preparar la agenda para la reunión.
16. al banquero si el abogado pudo comprobar si la firma ha sido falsificada.
17. al arrendador si los inquilinos actúan como si fueran dueños.
18. al profesor si la consejera no cree si ese es un problema de largo alcance.
19. al tesorero cuándo recibiremos el último pagaré del Sr. Castro.
20. a la profesora qué decidió el comité en la reunión tan prolongada.

C. Here you are given statements that are the answers to certain questions. Your assignment is to formulate the questions for these answers.

Ex.: She arrived yesterday.   When did she arrive?

1. No, we don't retail.
2. No, as a plumber he is not very good.
3. Yes, she agrees with you.
4. No, he did not back up my statement.
5. No, thanks. I have had enough dessert.
6. Yes, he took maximum advantage of the situation.
7. About $1,000 a share.
8. We have been traveling during all this week.
9. The worker told the foreman he had lost the tools.
10. He wants to dispose of the garbage.
11. The hearing will be tomorrow.

12. Students of all political creeds participated in the parade.

13. I have been in Puerto Rico for two years.

14. The apartments were built by our company.

15. We met him first in 1960.

16. The building is divided into four sections.

17. The goods can be stored at the warehouse for a week.

18. The bookkeeper is called Mickey.

19. It is called "The students' Orientation Center."

20. The contractor applied for a building permit.

D. Here you are given the interrogative statements in Spanish. Your assignment is *to translate* them into English.

1. ¿Se ha retractado el testigo de sus manifestaciones?

2. ¿Han votado los trabajadores de la factoría?

3. ¿Se había esforzado el trabajador diestro en hacer lo mejor posible?

4. ¿Huyó el desconocido con una gran suma de dinero?

5. ¿Está el empleado haciendo espacio para la nueva mercancía?

6. ¿Discuten los inquilinos los puntos sobresalientes de la demanda?

7. ¿Estará la farmacia abierta pasado mañana?

8. ¿No tienen algunos de nuestros productos mercado en el extranjero?

9. ¿Tiene el consejero una idea clara del problema?

10. Si usted fuera abogado redactaría el testamento de ese modo?

11. Si el bombero hubiese estado en huelga, ¿hubiera ido a apagar el fuego?

12. ¿Habremos localizado el error mañana a las seis de la tarde?

13. ¿Habían estado los empleados de mantenimiento trabajando horas extra?

14. ¿No va nadie a protestar por el hacinamiento en las cárceles?

15. ¿Vino alguien a verme?

17. ¿Ha estado Juan hablando con su consejero?

18. ¿Toleraste todas las interrupciones?

19. ¿No había despegado el avión cuando te fuiste?

20. ¿Viene el contador de costo temprano todos los días?

E. Here you are given the question. Your assignment is *to supply the answer to each question, and then translate both the question and the answer.*

1. What is the gas price in that country?

2. What can you tell about the surgeon who will operate on my cousin?

3. When is the deadline for paying the premium on the policy?

4. Who did you you say was appointed president?

5. Who received the personalized checks?

6. How do you operate   this computer?

7. May I be considered an applicant for this job?

8. Why does the consulting firm charge so much?

9. Can he lend us the fire extinguisher?

10. Must he do without the supplies, or should I send him part of the requisition?

11. At which warehouse do you get the best service?

12. Would you ask for an exchange on the purchase if you were in her place?

13. How many persons applied for the job?

14. How often does your tenant call you up for repairs on the house?

15. How much do you want for your property?

16. Where is the list of merchants who inflated the prices?

17. Which radio programs do you prefer?

18. Could you enumerate the highlights of the speech?

19. Would you enumerate the highlights of the speech?

20. Had they had serious labor troubles before? Why?

F. Here you are given the declarative statements in Spanish. Your assignment is *to change them to question form in English.*

Example: El profesor que hace la investigación necesita los datos sin demora. Does the research professor need the data without delay?

1. Los gastos de reparación son $1,000.

2. La periodista ha leído la querella.

3. El ingeniero tiene la pieza de la máquina electrónica.

4. El experto detectó la firma falsificada.

5. Sus inquilinos son puntuales en sus pagos.

6. El pagaré vencerá el 10 del mes próximo.

7. La secretaria había asistido al seminario.

8. El estudiante iría a la actividad, si tuviese una invitación.

9. Los estudiantes han escrito una carta de reclamación.

10. Los planificadores no cumplieron su promesa.

11. Los peritos tasadores le darán a usted el valor real de su inmueble.

12. El no tenía información exacta sobre los últimos acontecimientos.

13. El cajero estaba cuadrando sus cuentas cuando yo entré.

14. El cliente desea conocer el precio de las propiedades muebles marcadas en la lista.

15. Los voluntarios que trabajan por el bienestar de los adictos a drogas hacen una labor encomiable.

G. *Here you are given the statement. Your assignment is to convert it into question form and translate both statement and question.*

1. *This is a cogent argument.*

2. *A new car uses more fuel during the break-in period.*

3. The clerk is making room for the new merchandise.

4. The merchant is not stocking up on scarce items.

5. The depositor does not want a transfer of funds.

6. The company could file charges against the employee.

7. The engineer took pains to finish the project on time.

8. The foreman did not report the absentees.

9. The personnel assistant has gone on a trip.

10. The graduates have filed job applications.

11. Those aliens have not acquired United States citizenship.

12. The farmer's land has yielded a good crop.

13. The masons had not used steel scaffolding before.

14. She has been trying to get the manager on the telephone for hours.

15. The trainee has not been doing her best.

16. The paymaster had been acting suspiciously.
17. The manager will file charges against the employee.
18. The Senior students shall have gone on a trip by this time next year.
19. If you were the defendant company, you would do likwise.
20. If she had been the speaker, she would have yielded the floor to me.

UNIT VI
COGNATES AND CONFUSING WORDS

Part 1   True Cognates
Part 2   Cognates with Variation of
          Meaning in Specific Contexts
Part 3   False Cognates
Part 4   Confusing Words
Part 5   Translation Exercises
          —Spanish to English
          —English to Spanish

COGNATES

Cognates are words with identical or similar form common to different languages. From a historical viewpoint, we might say that cognates reveal a common ancestry from a "parent" language. Cognates, therefore, are easily recognizable. They will either be A) identical in written form as in the English/Spanish examples -- AREA or SOCIAL: or B) similar in written form as in ACTIVE/ACTIVO or CIRCUMSTANCE /CIRCUNSTANCIA, with only a slight vowel or consonant variance in the words to fit the morphological patterns peculiar to English and Spanish.

When cognates not only have an identical or similar form but also a corresponding meaning in any two languages in question, they are referred to as "true". True cognates present no difficulty for language students because their meaning is always the same in all contexts in both languages.

Part I of this chapter presents a selected list in alphabetical order of *true cognates* in English and Spanish. This selection is arbitrary. Students might profitably prepare their own list of true cognates in English and Spanish in order to practice easy recognition and enlarge their own vocabulary. They will be aware, of course, that the spoken form of the cognates will follow the phonetic peculiarities of English and Spanish.

Not all cognates, however, are true. Where two different languages will retain identical or similar word forms, sometimes the meaning of certain cognates changes over the course of time in one or other of the languages. When a change in meaning occurs in only one of the languages in question, we are faced with a possibly deceptive or misleading cognate, often called "false".In other words, they look the same but have different meanings in both languages. Moreover, this difference in meaning is applicable to all contexts in which they appear; for example, "sympathetic" in English can never be substituted for "simpático" in Spanish. Observe the meaning of these adjectives in the following sentences:

a) The Management is *sympathetic* towards the workers' demands. La Gerencia *ve con buenos ojos* las exigencias de los trabajadores. (sympathetic - favorably disposed)

b) La secretaria es una persona *simpática*.
The secretary is a *pleasant* person. (simpática - agradable)

Among other examples we could cite are: "sensible" translated into Spanish as "juicioso", not "sensible", and "cándido" translated into English as "sincere", not "candid". We use the term "possibly deceiving" cognates because the only way the language learner can avoid the deception of "false" cognates is to know them well.

Part 2 of this unit presents some cognates that most commonly cause difficulties which arise when the cognate has a variation of meaning in specific contexts or situations. In the very first example of this list, ANNOUNCE and ANUNCIAR provide a true cognate in the context of a wedding; however, in the context of Marketing or Publicity, English "advertises" a product. Observe the same situation with example 17 from the list. A very common deception of this kind is seen with REALIZE/ REALIZAR. In English, "realize" normally means "darse cuenta". In Spanish, "realizar" carries the meaning "accomplish or carry out" (llevar a cabo). Nevertheless, in a business context, "to realize the merchandise" and "realizar la mercancía" have the same meaning in both languages. Part 2, then, will examine the semantic transformations of some of these cognates in specific contexts. A solid knowledge of the "idiom" of both languages is the ideal way to avoid errors in this aspect of cognate deception.

PART 1

TRUE COGNATES
(Identical in Written Form)

The Spanish and English terms in the list that follows have identical form and meaning in both English and Spanish. Notice that in some of the English cognates there is a slight difference in pronunciation

English	Spanish
1. adorable	adorable
2. auditor	auditor
3. agenda	agenda
4. ascension	ascensión
5. balance	balance
6. base	base
7. capital	capital
8. club	club
9. color	color
10. comparable	comparable
11. control	control
12. convertible	convertible
13. crisis	crisis
14. debate	debate
15. deficit	deficit
16. director	director
17. experimental	experimental
18. factual	factual
19. familiar	familiar
20. federal	federal
21. final	final
22. folio	folio
23. formal	formal
24. general	general
25. global	global
26. idea	idea
27. intellectual	intelectual

28. invite	invite
29. liberal	liberal
30. libido	líbido
31. local	local
32. marginal	marginal
33. natural	natural
34. normal	normal
35. personal	personal
36. portable	portable
37. popular	popular
38. prepare	prepare
39. radar	radar
40. radio	radio
41. real	real
42. rector	rector
43. record	récord
44. rival	rival
45. robot	robot
46. series	series
47. special	especial
48. suspension	suspensión
49. veto	veto
50. visual	visual

A. Prepare your list (not less than 25) of true cognates.

PART 2

COGNATES WITH VARIATION OF MEANING
IN SPECIFIC CONTEXTS

ENGLISH	SPANISH
1. *Announce*	*Anunciar*
to *announce* the sale	*anunciar* las rebajas
to *announce* the meeting	*anunciar* la reunión
to *advertise* the product	*anunciar* el producto
2. *Apply*	*Aplicar*
to *apply* the law	*aplicar* la ley
to *apply* one's knowledge	*aplicar los conocimientos*
to something	*de uno o solución de un*
problema to *apply* oneself	
to something	dedicarse, *aplicarse*
to apply for a position	*solicitar* un empleo
3. *Assist*	*Asistir*
to *assist* the manager in	*asistir* o ayudar al gerente
his work	en su trabajo
to *assist* a patient	*asistir* a un paciente
to *attend* the meeting	*asistir* a la reunión
4. *Canal*	*Canal*
the Panama *Canal*	el *Canal* de Panamá
Channel 4 on television	el *canal* 4 en televisión
official *channels*	*canales* oficiales
5. *Collection*	*Colección*
stamp *collection*	*colección* de sellos
collection of money	*recolección* o cobro de dinero
collective security	seguridad *colectiva*
collective bargaining	negociación *colectiva*
6. *Competence*	*Competencia*
his *competence* in the work	su *competencia* en el trabajo
the *competence* of a witness	la *competencia* de un testigo
to testify	para testificar (legal)
unfair *competition*	*competencia* desleal

7. Contribution	Contribución
your *contribution* to the fund	su *contribución* al fondo
your *contribution* to the	
magazine or newspaper	su *contribución* al periódico
	revista (artículos, poesías,
the income-tax return	*contribución* sobre ingresos
8. Demand (v) (require)	Requerir, demandar
Demand (n)	Demanda
work that *demands* patience	trabajo que requiere o
	(demanda) paciencia
supply and *demand*	oferta y *demanda*
offer price	precio de *demanda*
9. Direction	Dirección
to follow this *direction*	seguir esta *dirección*
the *address* on the letter	la *dirección* de la carta
10. Grade	Grado
the first *grade* in school	primer *grado* en la escuela
the Bachelor's *degree*	el *grado* de bachiller
a 60° *degree* angle	un ángulo de 60° *grados*
the *degree* of responsibility	el *grado* de responsabilidad
high *grades* in school	*notas* sobresalientes
	en la escuela
the *grade* of the road	el *declive* de la carretera
the *grade* of the goods	la *calidad* de la mercancía
11. Honor	Honor
to *honor* a check	*honrar* un cheque
to bestow an *honor*	otorgar un *honor*
upon a person	a una persona
to *honor* an agreement	*honrar* un acuerdo (cumplir o
	respetar un acuerdo)
the family *honor*	el *honor* de la familia
to have the *honor* of	tener el *honor* de ser
being chosen for ...	escogido para ...
12. Invertion	Inversión
invertion of the sentence	*inversión* de las partes
elements	de la oración
investment of the capital	*inversión* del capital
capital *investment*	*inversión* capital
13. Labor	Labor
the *labor* costs	costo de la *labor* o
	mano de obra
to *labor* in vain	*laborar* o trabajar en vano
a *labor*-saving	aparato que ahorra
device	*labor* (trabajo)

labor force	personal *obrero*
to be in *labor*	estar *de parto*

14. *Liquid* — *Líquido*
    liquid food — alimento líquido
    to *liquidate* a debt — *liquidar* una deuda
    liquid assets — valores que se pueden convertir en "cash", en *líquido*

15. *Pass* — *Pasar*
    to *pass* a subject in school — *pasar* o aprobar una asignatura
    to *pass* a law — *pasar* o aprobar una ley
    to *pass* for being somebody else — *pasar* por ser otra persona
    to pass over — *pasar* por alto, no hacerle caso

16. *Passive* — *Pasiva*
    the *passive* voice — voz *pasiva*
    the *passive* assets — valores *pasivos* (que no se pueden volver en cash (líquido) fácilmente, se dice también activos, intangibles
    a *passive* person — persona *pasiva* (que no es activa)

17. *Realize* — *Realizar*
    to *realize* all the merchandise — *realizar* (vender) toda la mercancía
    to *realize* the project of one's preference — *realizar* (llevar a cabo) el proyecto de la preferencia de una persona

18. *Retire* — *Retirar*
    to *retire* from business — *retirarse* de los negocios
    to *withdraw* money from the bank — *retirar* dinero del banco

19. *Service* — *Servicio*
    secret *service* — *servicio* secreto (de contraespionaje)
    public *service* — *servicio* público
    to do someone a *service* — prestar *servicio* a uno

20. Terms
    to translate the English *terms* into French
    to be on good *terms* with
    the terms of the contract

Términos
    traducir los *términos* del inglés al francés
    estar en buenos *términos con*
    los términos del contrato

PART 3
FALSE COGNATES

False or deceiving cognates are words that have the same root, but different meanings in two languages (In our case Spanish and English). Since these words look alike, they are often treacherous and many times cause problems to the Spanish-Speaking student.

The sentences below illustrate the meaning of the cognates used. Study these carefully and write ten sentences using the cognates you find most difficult.

English	*Spanish*

1. ACT

The Jones *Act* was passed on March 2, 1917. It provided a civil government for Puerto till July 25, 1952 when the Constitution of the Commonwealth (ELA) was enacted.	El *Acta Jones* se pasó en marzo 2, 1917. Esta proveía un gobierno civil para Puerto Rico hasta el 25 de julio de 1952 cuando se puso en vigor la Constitución del Estado Libre Asociado.

ACTO

Act I of "My Fair Lady" was most interesting.	El acto I de "My Fair Lady" fué muy interesante.

2. ACTION (acción)

His *actions* brought him trouble.	Sus *acciones* le causaron problemas.

ACCION (Share or stock in a company)

I bought 100 *shares in the San Juan Racing Corporation.*	*Compré cien acciones* en la San Juan Racing Corporation.

3. ACTUAL (real)

We don't know the *real* reason for the personnel manager's resignation.

Ignoramos la *verdadera* razón de la renuncia del gerente de personal.

ACTUAL (en el presente)

At present (currently, right now, at the moment, at the present time) we process the orders according to date and time received.

Actualmente procesamos los pedidos de acuerdo con la fecha y hora que los recibimos.

4. CANDID (frank, sincere)

The doctor advised his patient to answer each question *candidly* or else he could not help her.

El doctor le aconsejó a su paciente que le contestara con *honestidad (francamente)*, de lo contrario él no podría ayudarla.

CANDIDO (without guile, naive)

The child was so *innocent* that he believed what the clown was telling him.

El niño era tan *inocente*, sin malicia, que creyó todo lo que el payaso le estaba diciendo.

5. CASUALTY (víctima, herido)

There were seven *casualties in* in the fire.

Hubo siete víctimas en el fuego.

CASUALIDAD (by chance)

I learned of the accident by mere chance.

Me enteré del accidente por mera *casualidad*.

6. *COMMODITY (movable goods that can be bought or sold)*

Speculators watch closely the price fluctuations of commodities.

Los especuladores están atentos a las fluctuaciones de precio de los artículos comerciales.

COMODIDAD

The house is high priced because it has a lot of comforts you can enjoy.

El precio de la casa es alto porque tiene muchas comodidadidades las cuales usted puede gozar.

7. CONFERENCE

Our two delegates to the convention are in *conference
now.*

Nuestros dos delegados a la
convención están en
conferencia ahora.

CONFERENCIA (lecture)

Please tell me the highlights of
the *lecture* delivered by the
computer expert.

Por favor dime los puntos
sobresalientes de la *conferencia* dictada por el experto en
computadoras.

8. CONFORM (to comply with
the rules)

To be successful, an employee
must *conform* to the rules
of his company.

Para tener éxito, un empleado
debe *obedecer* o *seguir*
las normas de su compañía.

CONFORMARSE

The votes reveal that the dissi-
dent group will have *to abide
by* the decision of the majority.

Los votos revelan que el grupo
*disidente tendrá que acatar la
decisión* de la mayoría (conformarse con).

9. DISGRACE (vergüenza)

The man's behavior is a
disgrace to his family.

La conducta de ese hombre es
una *desgracia* para su familia.

DESGRACIA (tragedia,
desastre)

The flood caused by the heavy
rains was a *disaster* for the
farmers.

La inundación causada por las
lluvias torrenciales fue un
desastre (desgracia) para los
agricultores.

10. EMBARRASSED (turbado,
avergonzado)

The messenger was
*embarrassed when the
secretary caught* him reading
the letter.

El mensajero se *avergonzó
cuando la secretaria lo sor-
prendió* leyendo la carta.

EMBARAZADA (pregnant)

The nurse took the *pregnant*
lady immediately to the labor
room.

La enfermera llevó a la señora
embarazada inmediatamente
al salón de parto.

11. EXIT (a going out, place of departure, any departure (hacer mutis)

The building has ten clearly marked emergency *exists*.	El edificio tiene diez *salidas de emergencia* claramente marcadas.

EXITO

The student's *success* in his college studies earned him praise from all his classmates.	El *éxito* del estudiante en sus estudios universitarios le ganó el elogio de todos sus compañeros.

12. FABRIC (woven, knitted or felted cloth)

In China one can get very beautiful fabrics for ladies' dresses.	En China, se puede conseguir *telas* muy bonitas para confeccionar trajes de señora.

Note: Factory in Spanish is "fábrica" which tends to confuse Spanish Speaking people. For example: "This *fabric* is out of stock" is often translated as "Esta *fábrica* está agotada."

FABRICA

The shoe *factory* workers were on strike because of the working conditions.	Los trabajadores de la *fábrica* de zapatos estaban en huelga debido a las condiciones de trabajo.

13. FIRM (compañía, empresa)

The two *firms* merged to avoid going bankrupt.	Las dos *firmas* se fusionaron para evitar ir a la bancarrota.

FIRMA (signature)

One of the *signatures* on this contract is almost illegible.	Una de las *firmas* en este contrato es casi ilegible (que no se puede leer).

14. LIBRARY

The books at the *Public Library* are for every body to read; so take good care of them.	*Los libros de la Biblioteca Pública* son para que todo el mundo los lea y disfrute; por lo tanto, cuídelos.

LIBRERIA

| When the books at the bookstores are classified by "subject matter" it is easy to find the book desired if it is in stock. | Cuando en las *librerías los* libros están clasificados por "materia" se hace fácil encontrar el libro deseado si lo tienen en almacén. |

15. NOMINATION (propose somebody as a candidate)

| There are two *nominations* for the position. | Hay dos *nominaciones* para el puesto. |

NOMBRAMIENTO (appointment)

| When the meeting adjourned, the President of the Council had not been *appointed* yet. | Cuando se levantó la sesión, el Presidente del Consejo no había sido *nombrado* todavía. |

16. QUIT (dejar de, abandonar)

| Because of her pregnancy and allergy, the lady had *to quit smoking.* | Debido a su embarazo y *alergias, la señora tuvo que dejar de* fumar. |

Quitar (remove)

| It isn't worthwhile *to remove* the furniture from that office. | *No vale la pena quitar* los muebles de esa oficina. |

17. QUOTE (citar, poner entre comillas)

| Enclose in quotation marks the part you *quote* from the treasurer's report. | Escriba entre comillas la parte que *cita* del informe del tesorero. |

COTIZAR (to quote a price)

| The prices the merchant *quotes on furniture sets are* too high. | Los precios que el comerciante *cotiza* por juegos de muebles son muy altos. |

18. SECURITIES (valores bursátiles)

| Bonds and shares are *securites.* | *Los bonos y las acciones son valores bursátiles.* |

SEGURIDAD (safety)

| *When there is an impending hurricane, one must take strict safety measures.* | Cuando se avecina un huracán, uno debe tomar medidas estrictas de seguridad. |

19. *SENSIBLE (possesing common sense or reason)*

That public relations manager is an asset to his company because he is very sensible.	*Ese gerente de relaciones públicas es valioso para su compañía porque es muy sensato.*

SENSIBLE (sensitivo, se ofende fácilmente)

She will never succeed as coordinator in her firm because she is very sensitive.	*Ella nunca tendrá éxito como coordinadora en su firma porque es demasiado sensible (impresionable).*

20. SYMPATHETIC (inclined to sympathy, favorably disposed)

In times of sorrow there are people who are more *sympathetic* with us than others.	En tiempos de dolor, hay personas que se *compadecen* de uno más que otras.

SIMPATICO (agradable)

The secretary is a *pleasant* nice young woman.	La secretaria es una joven *simpática* (agradable).

21. SYMPATHIZE (feel sorry for someone's misfortune)

I *sympathize* with those who lost their ones in the fire.	Me *compadezco* de todos aquellos que perdieron a sus seres queridos en el fuego.

SIMPATIZAR

The agency employees like the sales manager because he is very congenial.	*Los empleados de la agencia simpatizan con el gerente de ventas porque es muy afable.*

22. SYMPATHY (solidaridad) (feeling that which another feels)

I am in *sympathy* with him regarding the fringe benefits we should get.	*Comparto su criterio* en cuanto a los beneficios marginales que debemos obtener.
I wish to extend my *sympathy* to you because of your sorrow.	*Deseo darle el pésame* por su pena.

SIMPATIA

(friendliness)

When I went to the interview, I was nervous but Mr. Peppers *made me at ease.*

Estaba nerviosa cuando fui a la entrevista pero la *simpatía* de *Mr. Peppers me tranquilizó.*

PART 4
CONFUSING WORDS

The following words are grouped together for the purpose of illustrating differences existing between them. The spelling, pronunciation, meaning and difference in grammatical usage are factors that lead the majority of Spanish speaking students astray when using these terms.

Translate each expression into Spanish and notice the differences in spelling, pronunciation, meaning and grammatical usage.

1.	aboard	*aboard* the plane, ship or train
	abroad	working, studying or traveling *abroad* .
2.	assure	to *assure* proper credit
	insure	to *insure* valuable property.
3.	accountant	The *accountant* audits the books.
	bookkeeper	The *bookkeeper* keeps the books.
4.	addressee	The *addressee* receives the letter.
	addresser	The *addresser* sends the letter to the *addressee.*
5.	adopt	to *adopt* a child, to *adopt* a method
	adept	*adept* at swimming, adept at figures
	adapt	to *adapt* yourself to the conditions
6.	after	*after* me, *after* office hours
	behind	*behind* me, *behind* the counter
7.	along	*along* the road, to get *along* with people, *all along.*
	alone	to be *alone.*
8.	amount	the *amount* of money, the *amount* of supervision.
	quantity	a small *quantity* of milk, a quantity of fruit anything in bulk is *quantity.*

9.	bookstore	to buy books at the *bookstore*
	library	to borrow books from the *library*.
10.	brand (n.,v.)	a *brand* of liquor, medicine, or food
		to *brand* cattle.
	make	the *make* of a dress or an automobile
	mark	the *marks* in school, to use the wooden post as a *mark*.
11.	canvas (n., adj.)	a *canvas* for the oil painting, *canvas* shoes, a canvas tent
	canvass (v., n.)	to *canvass* a district for votes, to conduct a nationwide canvass of opinion, to make a *canvass* among the members
12.	capitol	the *capitol* building
	capital	the *capital* of Portugal, *capital* letter, *capital* punishment, a *capital* of $25,000, *capital* investment
13.	case	a *case* of wine
	box	a *box* of matches
	package	a *package* of cigarettes.
14.	cash (v.,n.)	to *cash* a check, to sell for *cash*
	change (v., n)	to *change* the title, to get *change* at the bank.
	exchange (v.,n.)	to *exchange* presents, to buy shares at the *exchange*, the rate of *exchange*.
15.	cashier	to ask the *cashier* for change
	paymaster	to ask the *paymaster* for your check
16.	compliment	He paid me a *compliment*. *complimentary* copies, *complimentary* close.
	complement (n.,adj.)	This angle is a *complement of the others*. *complementary* angles.
17.	corespondent	the *corespondent* in a divorce suit
	correspondent	the newspaper *correspondent*.
18.	costumer	The *costumer* deals in costumes.
	customer	He is a good *customer* of our store.
19.	costume (n.,adj.)	a native *costume*, *costume* jewelry
	custom (n., adj.)	a pleasing *custom* among Puerto Ricans, a national *custom*
	customs	*customs* duties.

20. council — The Student *Council*
    counsel (v.,n.) — to *counsel* a person, the prisoner's *counsel*, to give *counsel*.

21. couple — a German *couple*
    pair — a *pair* of scissors or shoes

22. courage — soldiers of *courage*
    angry — to be *angry* with a person, to be *angry* at a situation

23. dedicate — to *dedicate* a photo, to *dedicate* the book to a friend, *dedicated* to the production of citrus fruit
    devote (v., adj.) — to *devote* your time, a *devoted* mother

24. desert (v., n.) — to *desert* a wife
    the Sahara *desert*
    dessert — to eat *dessert* after lunch

25. destiny — It is her *destiny* to serve others.
    destination — port of *destination*

26. dictate — to *dictate* orders, to *dictate* letters
    deliver — to *deliver* a speech, to *deliver* an order or a package.
    The doctor *delivered* the baby.

27. earn — to *earn* a high salary, to *earn* a living, to *earn* honors, to *earn* a degree.
    win — to *win* the contest, to *win* $50 at the horse races, to *win* over the "San Juan" team
    gain — to *gain* $500 in the transaction
    to *gain* weight, to *gain* fluency of speech
    beat (v., n.) — to *beat* the team, to *beat* eggs, the heart beat

28. economic — the *economic* condition of Puerto Rico
    economical — to be *economical*
    economics — to study *economics*
    economy — the world *economy*

29. eligible — an *eligible* applicant, *eligible* for parole
    legible — a *legible* document or handwriting
    illegible — an *illegible* signature
    ineligible — to be *ineligible* for a position
    to be *ineligible* for the competition

125

30. enjoy	to *enjoy* yourself at the party
divert	to *divert* the plane to Havana, to *divert* one's attention from one's work
31. explode	to *explode* the homemade bomb
exploit	to *exploit* the uninformed citizen
32. finger	to wear a ring in one's *finger*
toe	a shoe that hurts one's *toes*
33. flee (v.)	Some revolutionaries will *flee* the country to avoid being caught.
fly (v.,n.)	An airplane *files* smoothly in good weather.
	Flies are dangerous insects.
34. foreigne.	the passport for the *foreigner*
stranger	the directions for the *stranger*.
35. game	the baseball *game*, the wild *game* of the African jungle
gamble	to *gamble* at the casino
play	to *play* cards, to *play* the piano.
36. guard	to *guard* the exit, to mount *guard*
keep	to *keep* the secret.
37. holy day	Good Friday is a *holy day*.
holiday	Armistice Day is a *holiday*.
vacation	a month's *vacation*
38. lecture	the *lecture* given by the scientist
conference	a press *conference*, the annual *conference* of dealers
39. lose	to *lose* money gambling
loose	to *loose* the knot, a *loose* knot, *loose* information, a *loose* translation
loss	a financial *loss*
miss	to *miss* the bus, to *miss* a person
40. major (n., adj.)	a *major* in the army, *major* subject, *major* groups of investments, *major* airlines
mayor	the *mayor* of San Juan
41. must (aux. v.,n.)	You *must* go. It is a *must*. I do not like *must*.
most	*most* people
42. name	to *name* the baby Mary, to be *named* the best travel writer of the year

	to be *named* to receive the academy highest award
nominate	to *nominate* for the presidency
appoint	to *appoint* as president
43. note	to write a *note*, a bank *note*, a *note* of concern in a person's voice
grade	to get a low *grade* in school
44. notice (v.,n.)	to *notice* her manners, the *notice* on the bulletin board, to read the *notice*
news	What is the latest *news*? to read the *news*
45. personal	*personal* remark, *personal* property
personnel	*personnel* management, *personnel* officer
46. prescription (n., adj.)	the doctor's *prescription*, the *prescription* book
recipe (n., adj.)	The *recipe* for baking a cake, the *recipe* book
receipt (n., adj.)	to acknowledge *receipt*, a *receipt* book
47. principal	the *principal* of the school, the safety of the *principal* investment
principle	the *principle* of truth, philosophical *principles*
48. proceed	to *proceed* with a speech
proceeds	the *proceeds* of the game, the *proceeds* of the business
precede (v., adj.)	to *precede* someone, the *preceding* chapter
49. realize	to *realize* the danger, to *realize* a profit
recognize	to *recognize* a man, to *recognize* a signature
50. resign	to *resign* a job, a blind *resignation* to a mother's authority, to *resign* to one's bad luck
renounce	to *renounce* a claim
51. respectively	her brother and son *respectively*
respectfully	*respectfully* submitted to the president
52. safe (adj., n.)	a *safe* place, a *safe* in the bank
save	to *save* money, to *save* a person

53. seal	to *seal* the letter, to *seal* a deed, Christmas *seals*, the *seal* of Puerto Rico
stamp	to *stamp* his signature, to *stamp* the letter, a five-cent *stamp*
54. scriptures	the Holy *Scriptures*
deeds	to register the *deeds* of sale, to justify his *deeds*
55. source	*diplomatic sources*, tax paid at the *source*
fountain (adj., n.)	*fountain* pen, water *fountain*
56. station	the railway *station*, the radio *station*
season (n., adj., n.)	the summer *season*, the hunting *season*, *seasonal* jobs, *seasoned* traveler, to *season* meat with salt and pepper
57. steal	to *steal* money or jewelry
rob	to *rob* a bank or a person
rub	to *rub* your skin
58. strike (v., n.)	to *strike* a balance, to *strike* a person, to go on *strike*
stroke (v., n.)	to *stroke* a baby, two *strokes*, to have a *stroke*
59. subject	*the subjects* in the curriculum the *subject* under discussion
signature	illegible *signature*
60. swatch	a *swatch* of silk or linen
sample	a *sample* of food, medicine or perfume
61. tear (v.,n.)	to *tear* a paper or a dress, a *tear* in her dress, the baby's *tears*
break	to *break* a piece of wood, to *break* the news, to *break* into a room, to *break* in a secretary, to *break* down into tears, to *break* a law, to *break* up a strike
62. touch (v., n., adj.)	to *touch* a person, the personal *touch*, to keep in *touch* with a person, the ship *touching* at many ports
play (v., n.)	to *play* the piano, to *play* a part, to *play* cards, to say a thing in *play*
63. use	to *use* paint, to *use* ink
wear	to *wear* a dress, lipstick or perfume

PART 5
TRANSLATION EXERCISES
SPANISH TO ENGLISH

These sentences contain some of the most common of the Words Confused and Cognates you have studied in this unit. When doing the translation, watch for the deceptive cognates and verb tenses.

1. La cajera se da cuenta de que al revelar la causa de su renuncia, la junta procederá inmediatamente a investigar el caso. Ella tenía en mente entablar una demanda contra la companía.

2. Con la muestra de harina que me regaló el vendedor extranjero, preparé una receta de bizcocho con especies que es riquísimo.

3. El pagador acostumbra ahorrar el dinero que gana trabajando horas extras y el que se gana haciendo pequeñas transacciones, para pagar las contribuciones de su casa.

4. Cuando supimos la noticia de que habían nombrado el nuevo alcalde, nos alegramos porque vimos que nuestra campaña tuvo éxito.

5. El técnico de laboratorio pasó sus vacaciones estudiando para tomar exámenes de dos asignaturas en las que había obtenido notas deficientes.

6. Los ladrones que asaltaron el banco robaron una cuantiosa suma y ni siquiera los guardianes se dieron cuenta.

7. Te echaremos de menos, pero sabemos que te divertirás mucho entre tantos jugadores profesionales de póker.

8. El mensajero no pudo traerme menudo a causa de que el cajero se negó a cambiar el cheque porque la firma no se podía casi leer.

9. Este psicólogo ha dedicado muchos años a luchar por la abolición de la pena de muerte en su estado.

10. En el Canal 3 anuncian los productos que nos hacen competencia.

11. El periódico tiene una sección especial ilustrada dedicada a los deportes.

12. Los ejecutivos requieren en sus subalternos, como cualidades principales, la competencia y la lealtad.

13. Cuando hay recesión, las cobranzas locales y las extranjeras son lentas.

14. El punto de destino del barco es Génova, pero antes hará escala en varios puertos.

15. A bordo del barco iban unos "hippies" que usaban ropa rota y muchísimos collares.

ENGLISH TO SPANISH

1. One of the airports in New York was named after John F. Kennedy.

2. When the fire broke out, everybody headed for the fire-exit stairs.

3. When I went on vacation last year, I was afraid somebody would divert the plane to Havana.

4. Attractive costume jewelry does a lot for a basic dress.

5. When the lawyer said his client should be eligible for parole, there was a note of concern in his voice.

6. The ceremony for the dedication of a federally subsidized project was the principal event of the day.

7. The lawyer demands that two interpreters assist him in the lawsuit against the two foreigners.

8. I know the brands of perfumes she sells, but I can't tell you the make of dresses she promotes.

9. She is very resourceful. For example, she is adept at preparing numerous French and Italian recipes.

10. The entertainment program is designed to divert the people's attention from their economic problems.

11. Some of the signatures of the signatories of the legal document were almost illegible.

12. The immigration Department is trying to control the illegal entry of Mexican aliens at their source of entry.

13. The trainees labor hard to achieve their goal.

14. The supply and demand affect the price of a product.

15. The Boy Scouts conducted a massive canvassing of the area in hopes of locating the missing child.

16. During his travels abroad the newspaper correspondent met very interesting people.

17. When returning from a foreign country, we have to go through customs.
18. The purchasing manager has made many investments abroad.
19. The student played the piano so beautifully that she earned a prize.
20. Their sympathies are with those workers who were laid off without previous notice.
21. It must be embarrasing to make commitments and not be able to comply with them later.
22. That politician's behavior is a disgrace to those citizens who voted for him.
23. The passengers saved their lives by using the exits as soon as they received the signal.
24. That action could affect the personnel manager's prestige for he might be accused of breach of contract.
25. The offices we are selling you conform to all the requirements established by law.
26. The engineer will succeed beacacuse he is a hard-working sensible person.
27. The investors have to be very careful when they are going to invest a large amount of money in securities.
28. In a press conference, the mayor said he would do his best to live up to the expectations of those who elected him.
29. That family had four casualties in yesterday's accident, so they have received hundreds of sympathy messages.
30. The store on the corner sells beautiful but expensive linen fabrics.
31. In spite of the business slowdown, our firm has a sale next week with attractive competitive prices.
32. The three nominations for the job have a solid business and cultural background.
33. Generally, we sympathize with people who have to meet a deadline to solve a difficult problem.
34. The speaker quoted a psalm from the Bible to emphasize his viewpoint.
35. Discouraged workers sometimes simply quit looking for jobs.

UNIT VII

PREPOSITIONS FUNCTION AND APPLICATION

Part 1   English to Spanish
Part 2   Near English Equivalents
Part 3   Spanish to English
Part 4   Omission of Prepositions

PREPOSITIONS: FUNCTION
AND APPLICATION

A preposition connects a noun or pronoun with another word or group of words. The choice of the preposition to be used is sometimes perplexing. If the wrong preposition is chosen, the meaning intended often changes. Futhermore, custom has established the use of certain prepositions with some adjectives and verbs, and the use of incorrect prepositional forms violates idiom, Idiom, as we know, refers to phrase combinations which are justified by custom rather than by logic or prescriptive grammar.

To learn expressions containing correct prepositional forms in a foreign language helps you to use that language fluently. The following examples will enhance your oral as well as written expression. This list includes many common expressions used in daily conversation and in business circles. These prepositional phrases are presented in context to help you grasp their meaning easily.

PART 1

ENGLISH TO SPANISH

1. abide by
acatar una cosa, mantenerla, obrar de acuerdo a ella

If you do not *abide by* your promise, you will get into trouble.

2. absent from
estar ausente de

Don't be *absent from* the meeting scheduled for Saturday.

3. abstain from
abstenerse de

Firms doing business with us should *abstain from* giving Christmas presents to agency personnel.

4. accompanied by (a person or animal)
acompañado de (persona o animal)

The suspect was *accompanied* in court *by* his brother and a lawyer.

5. accompanied with
acompañado de (un objeto)

Each proposal must be *accompanied with* a bid bond.

6. according to
según, conforme a

According to the reporter many legislators will abstain from voting on the project.

7. adapt for
adaptar para

The social worker's manners *adapt* her *for* winning the inmates' confidence.
Many classics have been *adapted for* all age levels.
The drama was *adapted for* musical comedy.

8. adapt from
inspirarse en, adaptar de

La Fontaine *adapted* the themes for his fables *from* Aesop's.

9. adapt to
ajustarse a, adaptarse a

Adapt yourself *to* the new schedule.

10. agree in (principle)   **concordar en**

I *agree* with the legislator *in* his opinion concerning unemployment compensation.

The council voted for the law although they do not *agree* with it *in* principle.

11. agree with   **concordar con, estar de acuerdo con, sentar bien**

Spicy foods usually do not *agree with* old people.

These fingerprints do not *agree with* the ones the police have in the laboratory.

Management *agreed with* the economist on his discussion of fringe benefits.

12. agree to (consent to)   **dar consentimiento, aprobar**

The two nations *agree to* the cease-fire treaty.

We may *agree to* something that we actually do not agree with.

13. agree upon, on   **aprobar, convenir en, ponerse (a plan or policy)**   **de acuerdo**

The senators have been unable to *agree upon* the redistribution plan for the funds.

The commission couldn't *agree on* how to broach the subject.

14. angry at   **enfadarse por (situation or condition)**

The merchant was *angry at* the delay of the goods.

15. angry with (a person)   **enfadarse con**

The mananger was *angry with* the mechanic because he appropriated the tools.

16. answer for   **ser responsable de, dar cuenta de algo a una persona, explicar**

All personnel will *answer to* me *for* the office property entrusted to them.

The student was unable to *answer for* his failure in the exam.

17. apologize for (a thing)   **presentar sus excusas por, disculparse con**

Please accept my *apology for* this belated expression of sympathy.

18. apologize to (a person)   **presentar sus excusas, disculparse con**

The editor *apologized to* the statistician for the misprint in the newspaper.

19. **appropriate for**   **apropiado para, destinar o**
    (a purpose or situation)   **asignar fondos para, útil para**

The new business office forms are *appropriate for* our particular interoffice needs.
The goverment will *appropriate* a large sum of money *for* subsidizing housing for the poor.

20. **appropriate from**   **apropiarse de**
    (an author)

The writer *appropriated* some ideas *from* the scientists' research paper.

21. **appropriate (to oneself)**   **apropiarse de**

The cashier *appropriated* the money and fled the country.

22. **approve of (a situation)**   **aprobar, dar por bueno, tener**
    opinión favorable

Some students do not *approve of* the new curriculum reorganization.

23. **argue about**   **discutir o disputar acerca de**

Several students *argued about* the new class schedules.

24. **argue against**   **hablar o argumentar en**
    contra de

Several student groups *argued against* the increase in the registration fee.

25. **argue for**   **argumentar o abogar a**
    favor de

Several student groups *argued for* student participation.

26. **argue with (a person)**   **discutir con, disputar con**

Mr. Benson was *arguing with* the chief executive officer when I entered.

27. **ask for**   **preguntar por, pedir**

    (a person or something
    desired)

We shall *ask for* product information before placing the order.

28. **ask about**   **pedir información acerca de**
    (a person, a thing)

The policeman was *asking about* the suspect's reputation.

29. **attend to**   **ocuparse de**
    (take care of)

Attend to the luggage while I get change.

30. bargain for   negociar para obtener algo, contar con

The rent was higher than I *bargained for.*

31. bargain with   regatear con

To *bargain with* some Italian merchants will increase your chances of getting your money's worth.

32. behalf of (on...of)   en nombre de todas, interceder por alguien

The secretary accepted the donation *on behalf of* the organization.
The manager interceded *on his behalf.*

33. bestow upon, on (persons)   otorgar, conferir

The Swedish Academy *bestows Nobel Prizes* on distinguished scholars.

34. borrow from   tomar prestado a
(persons, institutions)

The farmer intends to *borrow* $1,000 *from the bank to fight pests in his citrus plantation.*

35. compare with   comparar con
(show points of resemblance)

That doctor's fees were remarkably low *compared with* those in other parts of the country.

36. compare to (compare unlike   comparar con
objects for the purpose of
illustration)

The poet *compared* the color of her hair *to* the darkness of the night.

37. comply with   ajustarse a, obedecer

The regulations must specify which insular laws must be *complied with.*
These engines *comply with* federal standards.

38. concern about   inquieto por, preocupado por

The auditor's actions reflected *concern about* last year's loss.
The doctor is much *concerned about* the patient's health.

39. concerned with   se refiere a, trata sobre

The convention this year will be *concerned with* industrial relations.

40. concur in (an opinion)   **convenir en, estar de acuerdo con**

This commission *disagrees with* you concerning the end of work stoppage, but does *concur in* principle.
We *concur with* the committee in their desire to change the approach to the problem.

**41. concur with
(agree with a person)**   **estar de acuerdo con una persona**

The Chief Justice *concurred with* the investigators in their opinion of the inquest.

42. confer on (grant, bestow)   **conferir a, otorgar a**

The University *conferred* honorary *degrees on* various professors.

43. confer with (exchange views)   **cambiar de ideas, conferenciar sobre**

The agency heads *conferred with* the Governor on possible ways to minimize unemployment.

44. confide in   **confiar en, fiarse de**

The executive *confided in* his assistant, but later realized his mistake.

45. confide to (entrust to)   **encomendar a**

I will *confide to* you our marketing strategy.

46. congratulate on   **felicitar por**

I *congratulate you on* your election as president of our company.

47. convenient to (near)   **cerca de, accesible a**

Our hotel is *convenient to* the shopping center.

48. convenient for (a purpose)   **apropiado para, conveniente para**

The top floor is *convenient for* establishing a restaurant.

49. conversant with (versed in)   **versado en, experto en**

Diplomats *conversant with* Latin American affairs opposed cutting off financial aid to Nicaragua.

50. correspond to (to be similar)   **corresponde, de acuerdo con**

Part of the reports *corresponds to* the facts we already know.

51. correspond with   **tener correspondencia**
      (to communicate with some-   **con alguien**
      one in writing)

I *correspond with* foreign students; usually I receive two letters monthly.

52. deal in (to sell)   **comerciar en, vender**

They *deal in* real estate.

53. deal with (to have   **tratar sobre, tratar con,**
      to do with, subjects,   **ocuparse de**
      people)

This legislation *deals with* social security payments.
We *deal with* many Latin American bankers.
The special adviser *deals with* labor management relations.

54. depend on, upon   **contar con, confiar en,**
      (to rely, to trust)   **depender de**

Many residents of that small town *depend on* the factory for employment.

55. depend on, upon   **depender de**
      (to be contingent on)

Your salary will *depend on* your experience and preparation.

56. different from   **distinto a, diferente a,**
      discrepa de

Their attitude concerning the problem is *different from* ours.

57. differ from (in quality)   **no ser igual, ser diferente**

The workmanship on this sweater *differs from* what I expected.

58. differ from (to be unlike)   **no ser iguales, se diferencian**

The two lots differ from each other in size, shape, and price.

59. differ with (disagree in   **no estar de acuerdo con,**
      opinion)   **discrepar de**

The programmer *differed with* his boss regarding the interpretation of the speech.

60. enter in (the record)   **apuntar, anotar**
Enter in the minutes her opinion about why Mr. Sosa should be dismissed.

61. enter into (an agreement,   **llegar a un acuerdo, entablar**
      an alliance, a conversation,   **una conversación, etc.**
      a contract, discussion.

Yesterday, the two retailers *entered into an agreement* regarding sale prices.

62. enter upon   **emprender, comenzar**
    (to begin, to commence)

Many developing nations have *entered upon* a plan of mutual cooperation.

63. exception   **objetar, desaprobar**
    (to take exception to...)

The committee *took exception to* our point of view.

64. familiar with   **conocer, estar familiarizado**
                             con, estar enterado de

Become *familiar with* the operation of this microcomputer.

65. familiarize with   **familiarizarse con**

Familiarize yourself *with* people who have already adapted to that difficult situation.

66. free of, from   **libre de**

Proper safety measures will *free* the project *of* accidents.
Many adults seem to be *free from* inhibitions.

67. graduate from   **graduarse en**

The social worker *graduated from* Yale.

68. independent of   **independiente de,**
                             independizarse de

Their attempt to be *independent of* the union brought about trouble.

69. insist on, upon   **insistir en algo, empeñarse en**
                             hacer algo

The workers *insist on* getting higher pay.

70. interest in (v., n.)   **interesar en, interés en**

We would like to *interest* you *in* our far-reaching project.
I have no *interest in* buying long term bonds.

71. interest for   **interés por**

In this case the *interest for* three years is higher than I thought it would be.

72. interest rate on   **tasa de interés sobre**
                             préstamos

Our minimum *interest* rate on loans is ten percent.

73. mastery over (self)   **dominio de**

Mastery over your emotions is an asset when presenting controversial points.

74. mastery of   **dominio de**

His *mastery* of foreign affairs won him his high position.

75. monopoly in, of   **monopolio de**

Multinational companies have been accused of having the *monopoly* in some industries.

76. negotiate for   **negociar para obtener**
o conseguir

The stevedores are anxious to *negotiate for* a shorter working week.

77. negotiate with (people)   **negociar con**

The workers are interested in *negotiating with* the officers of the refinery.

78. operate on, for   **operar a, operar a uno de**

The surgeon will *operate on* the expectant mother.
The surgeon will *operate on* Mrs. Rivera *for* appendicitis.

79. part from   **separarse de uno, despedirse**
de uno

I *parted from* that company because of their unethical practices.

80. part with (money, property)   **desprenderse de**

I don't want to sell my old car. I wouldn't *part with* it for anything.

81. profit by (experience)   **beneficiarse de, sacar**
partido de

The new construction manager should *profit by* the new retirement system we have at present.

82. protect from   **proteger de**

New laws *protect* the consumer *from* misleading advertisements.

83. reconcile to (content with)   **resignarse a algo, conformarse**
con algo

The latest developments force us to become *reconciled to* the inevitable.

84. reconcile with   **reconciliarse con**
    (become friendly)

In politics leaders often engage in hot arguments, but they are soon *reconciled with* each other.

reconcile with (make   **hacer compatible o**
    compatible or consistent)   **consistente**

It is difficult to *reconcile her declaration with* what the letter states.

85. reputation for   **tener fama de**

She has a *reputation for* writing controversial editorials.

86. **subsccribe to (contribute, give support, approval)** **contribuir dinero para algo**

I *subscribe to* the Red Cross with $50 annually.

87. **substitute for** **sustituir, reemplazar**

We are not trying to *substitute* economic assistance *for* jobs.

88. **trample on, upon** **atropellar, maltratar, pisotear**

The majority should not *trample on* the rights of the minorities.

89. **vote down** **derrotar, rechazar por votación**

The proposal was *voted down.*

90. **vote for** **votar a favor de**

The committee *voted for* an increase in fees.

91. **vote in** **elegir (por votación)**

Our candidate was *voted in* at yesterday's meeting.

92. **vote on** **votar por**

We desire to *vote on* the motion.

93. **wait for** **esperar por**

Shall I *wait for* you here?

94. **wait on** **servir a, atender a**

Please *wait on* all students who have appointments.

95. **withdraw from** **retirar de**

Mrs. Rivera *withdrew* her son *from* school.
The training supervisor *withdrew* $200 *from* his account.

96. **working at** **trabajar en, ocuparse de**

The professor is *working at* his desk.

97. **work on** **trabajar en, (pintar, lijar, etc.)**

The carpenter is not *working on* the desk because he lost his tools.

98. **work for** **trabajar para**

The researcher is *working for* the United Nations.

99. **work with** **trabajar con**

The scientist is *working with* foreign colleagues on the project.

100. **worry about** **preocuparse por**

The production supervisor is *worried about* the wording in the report conclusions.

101. vary from   **variar de**

Merit systems *vary from* one company to another.

102. versed in   **versado en, ser conocedor de**

Diplomats are generally versed in various languages.

PART 2

NEAR ENGLISH EQUIVALENTS

Match the words in italics in Column A with their Near Equivalents in Column B.

A	B
a. I *rely on* your judgment.	___ 1. asking for information
b. They *have objected to* your viewpoints several times.	___ 2. was absent
c. The trainees *entered upon* their duties with enthusiasm.	___ 3. contribute
d. Those employees have *become reconciled to* their working conditions.	___ 4. contented with
	___ 5. trust me
e. Did María *become reconciled with* Juan?	___ 6. in favor of
f. The members of this department must attend the meeting because our candidate *should be voted in.*	___ 7. approve of
	___ 8. plagiarized
g. Can you *reconcile* her attitude *with* the statements in her letter?	___ 9. argue on the price
h. The employees voted *for* Mr. Stevens' candidacy.	___ 10. expecting
	___ 11. agreed with
i. That political party wanted me to *subscribe to* their fund with $100.	___ 12. exchanged views on
	___ 13. makes me sick
j. I am sure the committee will *vote down* the proposal.	___ 14. make up with
k. Many students do not *subscribe to* having the police on the campus.	___ 15. take care of
	___ 16. communicate in writing
l. Do you *correspond with* many people?	___ 17. opposed

m. That merchant *deals in* precious stones.

n. This dress *differs from* the one you bought at Padin's.

o. Do you *confide in* me?

p. I wasn't *bargaining for* that outcome.

q. Lobster doesn't *agree with* me.

r. The President *conferred a medal on* the soldier.

s. The company spokeswoman *consented to* the terms although she didn't like them.

t. Who was *asking about* me?

u. The nurse will *answer for* the child's welfare.

v. The police *concurred with* the detective, regarding the witness' reputation.

w. The trial was suspended because a witness *did not attend.*

x. *Attend to* the office while I am away.

y. *The student appropriated* two paragraphs from the article.

z. The budget chairman agreed with the president on the main issues.

aa. Secretaries *versed in* languages get attractive salaries.

bb. The managers *conferred on* the difficult situation.

cc. The authorities *are concerned about* air pollution.

dd. I dislike to *bargain with* the merchants at the "Plaza de Mercado."

_____ 18. trust

_____ 19. different from

_____ 20. be responsible for

_____ 21. elected

_____ 22. make consistent, compatible

_____ 23. began

_____ 24. concurred with

_____ 25. worried about

_____ 26. experts in

_____ 27. agreed to

_____ 28. *bestowed on*

_____ 29. sells

_____ 30. defeat

PART 3
SPANISH TO ENGLISH

Read the following sentences carefully. Then translate them and pay special attention to the terms in italics and to the verb tense.

1. Muchos jóvenes *insisten en independizarse* de sus padres; aún cuando dependen de éstos económicamente.

2. La mayoría de los trabajadores se *abstuvo de votar* porque rehusa *ratificar el contrato.*

3. *De acuerdo con las normas,* la propuesta debe venir *acompañada de un cheque* por mil dólares.

4. Es saludable *ajustarse a las circunstancias prevalecientes* y hacer lo mejor que se pueda.

5. La velocidad con que se producen los cambios en el mundo *impone un reto a todos nosotros.*

6. El gobierno está *insistiendo en* el derecho a suspender contratos con compañías que no estén *cumpliendo con las normas establecidas.*

7. *Felicité al cardiólogo que operó a mi amigo* tan exitosamente.

8. El Presidente estaba *acompañado del Secretario de Estado* cuando *objetó los comentarios del corresponsal.*

9. *Tenemos a su disposición* la casa que le conviene. *Esta es diferente a todas* las otras que usted ha visitado.

10. Los miembros de la junta *conferenciarán sobre los* puntos en disputa. Si llegan a un acuerdo, *lo anotaremos en el récord* para luego redactar el informe.

11. El corredor de bienes raíces radicó una demanda contra el dueño del edificio por *incumplimiento de contrato.*

12. Su ascenso *dependerá de su* dominio de las *relaciones obrero-patronales.*

13. *Benefíciese familiarizándose con* nuestro negocio de alquiler de automóviles.

14. A veces algunas personas *violan los derechos de sus vecinos.*

15. Los técnicos que tomaron el adiestramiento *se familiarizaron con* el manejo de la computadora.

16. El asistente *tiene interés en adquirir dominio de las nuevas técnicas de personal* para poder *beneficiarse de* los últimos principios gerenciales.

17. Me desagrada *negociar con* personas que faltan a la ética.

18. El *interés sobre esa cantidad de dinero, por tres años* es muy alto. Por esto, desisto de *tomar el dinero prestado a esa compañía financiera.*

19. Se acusó a un ingeniero de *apropiarse ilegalmente* de unos documentos oficiales de su compañía.

20. El ingeniero de seguridad *está preocupado por* las condiciones poco satisfactorias del andamiaje. Por esto le estamos enviando un *sustituto para* la pieza que nos solicitó.

21. A muchos de los miembros de la asamblea no les agrada la moción. *Imagino que la derrotarán.*

22. Al empezar el semestre, generalmente los estudiantes *comienzan sus labores* con entusiasmo.

23. La profesora estaba *incomodada por la contestación del estudiante. Luego éste se disculpó con ella.*

24. Los promotores del programa *recibieron felicitaciones por la excelencia de éste.*

25. El analista de costo que estaba *inquiriendo sobre usted* es uno de los que *abogaron por* la destitución del gerente de compras.

26. El corredor de inversiones *no estaba interesado en negociar con el presidente de la compañía de efectos eléctricos.*

27. *He diferido del portavoz de la compañía* varias veces, pero en este caso estoy de *acuerdo con él en principio.*

28. *De acuerdo con* la prueba que presentó el detective, las huellas que hay en la arena *no coinciden con* el tamaño del pie del niño perdido.

29. La casa exportadora nos pidió informes sobre la reputación del señor Sosa. *Le escribiré al señor Olmo* sobre el particular. También *consultaré a su jefe* anterior, ya que estoy *interesado en* presentar datos precisos.

30. Mi candidata es la *persona idónea* para llenar la vacante que tenemos. Baso mi criterio en lo siguiente:

    a. Su preparación *compara con* la que se exige en universidades de primera clase.

    b. *Domina la materia* en cuestión.

    c. *Está familiarizada* con la política internacional.

    d. *Tiene relaciones culturales y comerciales con instituciones muy conocidas.*

Sin embargo, *estoy preocupado por* la actitud que han asumido algunos socios de la compañía.

El discurso del presidente *trataba sobre el derecho de los estudiantes* a reunirse. Sin embargo, algunos estudiantes pronto *entablaron una discusión agria* y cuando llegó la policía muchos nos tuvimos que *proteger de ésta*. Al día siguiente leí en la prensa que varios espectadores *objetaron* la conducta de ambos grupos: la de la policía y la de los estudiantes.

PART 4

OMISSION OF PREPOSITIONS

Some words in Spanish require a following preposition, but in English their equivalents do not. Study carefully the sentences that follow. Then, write your own sentences in English.

1. *Abuse*

   The official abused his rights.

   El oficial abusó *de* sus derechos.

2. *Approach*

   Acercarse a

   They approached the tourists.

   Ellos se acercaron a los turistas.

3. *Ask* (a favor or request)

   Pedir a

   I asked the appraiser the evaluation of the property.

   Le pregunté *al* tasador el valor de la propiedad.

4. *Change*

   Cambiar de

   Why do you change cars now?

   ¿Por qué cambian *de* automóvil ahora?

5. *Concern*

   Concernir a

   His financial setbacks concern us.

   Sus reveses financieros nos conciernen. (a nosotros)

6. *Contribute*

   Contribuir con

   We wish to contribute books to the children's library.

   Deseamos contribuir *con* libros para la biblioteca de niños.

7. *Doubt*	*Dudar de*
The boss doubts her ability for that job.	El jefe duda *de* su habilidad para ese trabajo.
8. *Enjoy*	*Gozar de*
His professor enjoys a comfortable home in the country.	El profesor goza *de* de una casa cómoda en el campo.
9. *Enter*	*Entrar en*
The thieves entered the warehouse through an open window.	Los pillos entraron *al* almacén por una ventana abierta.
10. *Fulfill*	*Cumplir con*
If you fulfill your duty, you don't get in trouble.	Si cumples *con* tu deber no tienes problemas.
11. *Influence*	*Influir en*
The merchant tried to influence the student to buy a small computer.	El comerciante trató de influir *en* el estudiante para que comprase una computadora pequeña.
12. *Inside*	*Dentro de*
Your health certificate is inside the yellow box.	Su certificado de salud está dentro *de* la caja amarilla.
13. *Lack*	*Carecer de*
Some towns lack good public health services.	Algunos pueblos carecen *de* buenos servicios de salud pública.
14. *Match*	Hacer juego con
Her outfit doesn't match the occasion.	Su traje no es propio *para* la ocasión.
Her jewels don't match her dress.	Sus joyas no hacen juego *con* su traje.
15. *Marry*	*Casarse con*
The personnel officer will marry our secretary.	El jefe de personal se casará *con* nuestra secretaria.
16. *Meet*	*Encontrarse con*
They will meet me at the airport.	Ellos se encontrarán *conmigo* en el aeropuerto.

17. *Oppose*

The committee had opposed the president's former plan.

Oponerse a

El comité se había opuesto al plan anterior del presidente.

18. *Suspect*

The bank officials never suspected the receptionist.

Sospechar de

Los oficiales del banco nunca sospecharon de la recepcionista.

19. *Tell*

The prisoner told the prosecuting attorney everything about the plot.

Decir a, contar a

El prisionero contó al fiscal todo lo relativo a la conspiración.

20. *Resemble*

These adding machines resemble (look like) last year's.

Parecerse a

Estas máquinas de sumar se parecen a las del año pasado.

UNIT VIII
TIME EXPRESSIONS

Part 1   Reinforcement Exercises in
           Question-Answer Form
Part 2   Spanish to English
Part 3   English to Spanish

TIME EXPRESSIONS

Students are very often at a loss as to what to say in a given situation related with time. The following unit is designed to help you in the phrasing of your expressions of time in English.

In order to facilitate your learning of the expressions that follow, you are given both texts, Spanish and English, the first six parts being presented in question-answer form. Read both texts carefully and repeat them mentally as well as orally. Then proceed to write the translation in English for each expression in Spanish. In this way, you will become conversant with the phrases and you will master them so well that they will come to your mind automatically when you have to use them.

PART 1

REINFORCEMENT EXERCISES IN QUESTION-ANSWER FORM

A. ¿Qué hora es?

What time is it?

1. la una en punto — one o'clock sharp

2. la una menos cuarto — a quarter to one

3. la una y cuarenta — one forty, twenty to two, twenty minutes of two, twenty minutes before two

4. la una y cuarenta y cinco — one forty-five, fifteen of two

5. la una y cuarto — one fifteen, quarter past one, fifteen past one, a quarter after one

6. la una y media — one thirty, half past one

7. Mi reloj está adelantado. — My watch is fast.

8. Mi reloj está atrasado. — My watch is slow.

9. Mi reloj no marcha bien. — My watch doesn't run well.

10. Mi reloj se ha parado. — My watch has stopped.

11. Van a dar las cuatro. — It is almost four.

B. ¿Cuándo vienes a verme?

When are you coming to see me?

1. a fines de año — by the end of the year / at the end of the year

2. antes del obscurecer — before dark

3. dentro de pocos días — within the next few days

4. el 15 del mes próximo — on the 15th of next month

5. la semana después de la próxima — the week after next

6. mañana al amanecer — tomorrow at dawn, at daybreak

7. mañana a mediodía — tomorrow at noon, tomorrow noon

8. mañana al obscurecer — early tomorrow evening, at nightfall

9. mañana por la noche	tomorrow evening
10. mañana y pasado	tomorrow and the day after, tomorrow and the next day
11. pasado mañana en la madrugada	early in the morning, the day after tomorrow

C. ¿Desde cuándo ha estado él haciendo ese trabajo? — **Since when has he been doing that work?**

1. desde el 2 de noviembre	since November 2, since the second of November
2. por dos meses	for two months
3. por largo tiempo	for a long time
4. últimamente	lately

D. ¿Cuándo viene el distribuidor a visitarle? — **When does the distributor come to see you?**

1. algunas veces, a intervalos	off and on
2. a menudo	very often, frequently
3. a veces	sometimes
4. cada dos días	every two days
5. cada dos semanas	biweekly
6. casi nunca	occasionally, almost never
7. de vez en cuando	once in a while
8. todos los meses, el día 15	on the 15th of every month
9. un día sí y otro no	every other day

E. ¿Cuándo llega el avión? — **When does the plane arrive?**

1. adelantado	ahead of time
2. a tiempo, a la hora señalada	on schedule, on time
3. con retraso	behind schedule, behind time, late
4. de un momento a otro	at any time now, any minute now

F. ¿A qué hora salen los autobuses? — **What are the bus departure hours?**

1. De Boston a La Guardia: cada hora, desde las 7:30 a.m. hasta las 10:30 p.m.	From Boston to La Guardia: every hour on the half hour, from 7:30 a.m. to 10:00 p.m.

2. Para Newark: cada hora, desde las 7:00 a.m. a las 10:00 p.m.

To Newark: every hour on the hour, from 7:00 a.m. to 10:00 p.m.

3. Para Washington: una hora si y otra no, desde las 7:30 a.m. hasta las 10:30 p.m.

To Washington: every other hour on the half hour from 7:30 a.m. to 10:30 p.m.

PREPOSITIONS USED WITH EXPRESSIONS OF TIME

ON

on June 26, 1985
on the minute (to express punctuality)
on the 30th
on Sunday
on Sunday afternoon
on Sunday evening
on Sunday morning
on Sunday night
on the 7th of June

AT

at noon
at nightfall

at two o'clock
at noon yesterday
at dawn
at noon tomorrow
at midnight
at night
at five in the morning

IN

in June
in the afternoon
in the evening
in the future
in the morning
in the past
in the winter

in the summer
in the autumn
in the Middle Ages
in twenty minutes
in the fall
in 1980
in the eighteenth century

I. Use IN, FOR, BY, UNTIL, SINCE, AT, ON, in the following sentences:

1. These unemployed worked _____ six months last year.

2. The student has been absent from class _____ Monday.

3. Our office will announce the layoffs some time _____April.

4. The news will not be broadcasted _____later tonight.

5. We shall hold our convention _____ the spring.

6. The President's speech will not be ready _____ eight o'clock tomorrow morning.

7. _____ Saturday morning, I shall map out our activities.

8. The exhibition of the IBM's information processor shall be _____ 9 o'clock, April 20.

9. The working schedules should be ready _____ ten o'clock tomorrow morning.

10. _____ the future, please attend meetings regularly.

IDIOMS. TRANSLATE THESE SENTENCES

1.	as before	*As before,* we shall send you quarterly reports.
2.	at a time	The foreman dismissed the workers two *at a time.*
3.	at last	*At last,* the technician saw my point of view.
4.	at once	They all departed *at once.*
5.	at one time	*At one time,* the young man had many debts.
6.	at that time	*At that time,* our company made rocket engines for other companies.
7.	at the same time	Both guests arrived *at the same time.*
8.	at times	*At times,* we confuse the issues being discussed.
9.	day in, day out	*Day in and day out,* you can hear them arguing on the same problem.
10.	day of grace	The premium is due on the first of December, but the company grants you fifteen *days of grace.*

11. forever	She is *forever* complaining about her work schedule.
12. for good	The patient stopped smoking *for good.*
13. for long	He didn't hold the job *for long.* (Occurs only in sentences with negative words.)
14. for once	*For once,* he was in time for his appointment.
15. for the first time	*For the first time* in two months, the campaign manager has complied with my request.
16. from now on	*From now on,* plan your budget ahead.
17. from time to time	We give the club members demonstrations *from time to to time.*
18. in no time	The driver returned the valuables *in no time.*
19. in succession	The prosecuting attorney brought up the point three times *in succession.*
20. in that case	*In that case,* I won't make an issue of the situation.
21. in the beginning	*In the beginning,* the witness distorted the facts.
22. in the end	*In the end,* they decided to call off the meeting.
23. in the long run	*In the long run,* they will approve of my marketing strategy.
24. in the meantime	*In the meantime,* let's wait to see what they have in mind.
25. in the nick of time	The truck driver swerved *in the nick of time.*
26. in time for	Please arrive *in time for* preparing the agenda.
27. of late	*Of late,* those employees have been very productive.

28. on occasions	*On occasions,* he participates in public debates.
29. on time	Don't slow down production, come *on time* to work.
30. out of date	That fashion is *out of date.*
31. overnight	Extra guards stayed *overnight* at the factory because of the disturbances.
32. over the weekend	The ghost writers prepared the president's speech *over the weekend.*
33. sooner or later	*Sooner or later* she will agree on all the points.

MISCELLANEOUS

1. a altas horas de la noche	late at night
2. al ponerse el sol	at sunset
3. al salir el sol	at sunrise
4. anteayer	the day before yesterday
5. Buenas noches	Good evening! (when greeting or arriving)
6. Buenas noches	Good night! (when leaving)
7. cada hora en punto	every hour on the hour
8. después de la medianoche	after midnight
9. durante las 24 horas del día	around the clock
10. el año antepasado	the year before last
11. el año bisiesto	leap year
12. en la madrugada	at dawn, in the early morning, in the early hours, before sunrise
13. hace una semana	a week ago
14. hoy día	nowadays
15. la semana anterior a la pasada	the week before last
16. por toda la vida	for life
17. recién construída	newly-built
18. recién venidos	newcomers
19. una quincena	a fortnight

20. un asunto que tomará
    todo el día   an all-day affair

TECHNICAL TERMS

1. boleta de sueldo ganado	time ticket
2. carta de crédito a plazo	time letter of credit
3. depósito a tiempo fijo	time deposit
4. flete por tiempo	time charter
5. fondos para prestar a plazos	time money
6. gastado por el tiempo, fuera de moda	worn out, old-fashioned
7. giro a plazo	time draft
8. hoja de jornales devengados	time sheet
9. investigación del tiempo necesario para varias tareas (usado en la industria)	time study
10. itinerario, horario guía	timetable
11. letra a plazos o a término	time bill
12. libreta de jornales	time book
13. listero, alistador de tiempo	timekeeper
14. métodos que ahorran tiempo	time-saving
15. póliza de plazo fijo	time policy
16. rebaja por pago dentro del plazo especificado	time discount
17. reloj registrador	time clock
18. tarjeta donde se registran las horas trabajadas	timecard
19. tiempo extra	overtime
20. tiempo y medio	time and a half
21. tomador de tiempo	time clerk

NOUNS EXPRESSING TIME IN VARIOUS ASPECTS

Plazo- a period of time agreed upon

1. acortar un plazo	to shorten a term
2. alargar un plazo	to extend a term

3. a plazos cortos	in short-term installments
4. corto plazo	short term
5. el plazo y lugar convenidos	at the time and placed agreed upon
6. plazo fijo de 30 días	terms, 30 days
7. plazo señalado	stipulated date
8. Se ha cumplido el plazo.	The term has expired.
9. señalar un plazo	to set a time
10. vender a plazos	to sell on the installament plan

FOR IN EXPRESSIONS OF DURATION OF TIME MAY BE TRANSLATED AS: *hacia, hace, desde, por, durante, en, por espacio de.*

Notice the translation of the expressions in italics in the following sentences.

1. The secretary typed the lease *for the last time.*
   (por última vez)
2. He was head of the company *for years.*
   (durante muchos años, por años)
3. The student hasn't attended class *for a week.*
   (en una semana)
4. The operation on my sister *lasted for more than two hours.*
   (duró más de dos horas)
5. For how long has she been ill?
   (desde cuándo)
6. *He had been ill for three days.*
   (Hacía tres días que estaba enfermo.)
7. The stevedores refuse to work *for the duration*
   (por la duración de la huelga)
   (mientras dure la huelga)

PART 2
SPANISH INTO ENGLISH

The sentences that follow contain some of the expressions of time you have already studied. As you translate, pay special attention to the expressions in italics.

1. *Anteayer* celebramos el *quincuagésimo* aniversario de nuestra empresa.
2. Mi reloj *no funciona*, pero creo que son *las cinco menos diez.*
3. *Pocas veces* ese departamento envía el material *por adelantado.*
4. *En aquella época* no había procesadoras de palabras.
5. Tu presencia nos es muy grata, sin embargo son *raras* las veces que te vemos por aquí.
6. *Mañana* hace dos años que terminamos de construir la casa.
7. ¿Cuánto tiempo hace que usted paga contribuciones?
8. *Hace cuatro días* le reembolsamos $10, el importe de la rebaja por *el pago adelantado.*
9. Publicamos folletos ilustrados *cada tres meses,* en vez de *dos veces al año.*
10. Agradeceremos que presente por radio el anuncio de nuestros productos *cada hora,* desde las *siete en punto de la mañana* hasta las *diez de la noche.*
11. El año *antepasado* rendíamos los informes a la oficina central *cada quince días.*
12. *El 10 de agosto* o sea *dentro de una semana,* recibiremos los trajes de última moda.
13. *Cada dos días* el capataz nos envía *la hoja de jornales devengados.*
14. Si trabajamos *después de las cuatro y media,* devengaremos *jornal por tiempo y medio.*

15. ¿*Cuánto tiempo* hace que el mediador te escribió informándote que iba a acelerar la solución del problema?

16. Continúa haciendo ese trabajo, porque *durante el tiempo muerto* no habrá tarea para todos.

17. El *plazo que convinimos se ha cumplido,* por lo tanto le agradeceremos que se comunique con nosotros.

18. No podrá darme la información si no ha recibido la copia de la póliza de *plazo fijo.*

19. Estudie cuidadosamente la *tarjeta donde se registran las horas trabajadas* durante su tiempo libre, pues la discusión de *ese asunto* tomará *todo el día.*

20. *A más tardar mañana,* le enviaremos las cotizaciones que nos pidió *hace dos días.*

21. Aunque el autobus vino *con retraso* llegamos al aeropuerto a las *seis y veinticinco, a tiempo* para ver despegar el avión.

22. Creo que el avión viene a la *hora señalada,* pero es mejor que veas el *horario* en el tablón de edictos.

23. Las operarias deberán venir al taller *tres días corridos* para así reponer el *tiempo perdido* durante la huelga.

24. Para que puedas gozar de todos los privilegios, debes trabajar *tiempo completo* en vez de *tarea parcial.*

25. El Negociado del Tiempo predice *tiempo nublado* para *hoy por la mañana,* aguaceros dispersos para *la noche* y tiempo borrascoso para *mañana después de la puesta del sol.*

PART 3
ENGLISH INTO SPANISH

1. *The merchant is paying twelve percent interest on the time bill.*

2. The bookkeeper writes very neat figures in the *time book.*

3. If the company leases the boat, how much will they pay for the *time charter?*

4. When did the *time clerk* lose the record?

5. The *time clock* is out of order; therefore, you should take it to the IBM office.

6. Pay this obligation at the stipulated time so that you may get the *time discount.*

7. *Time drafts* or notes are payable at a stated period of time after they are presented.

8. The bearer of this *time letter of credit* will present it to the correspondent of the Chase Manhattan Bank in Spain.

9. Since Mr. Rivera is in charge of the *time money,* he can give you the information about loans.

10. The owner of the yacht bought an additional policy, a *time policy,* so it only covered thirty days.

11. *As soon as* we prepare the *time sheet,* you shall have the information you requested.

12. The Assistant Manager will meet with us tomorrow in order to discuss the results of the *time study.*

13. Tomorrow morning, at 9 o'clock, the systems analyst will lecture us on *time-saving* methods.

14. If you work *overtime* for three months, you will have money to pay your down payment on the electronics equipment you need.

15. During the coming week, we shall be so crowded with extra orders that we shall have to work *time and a half.*

UNIT IX
COMPUTER TERMS

Introduction

Part 1   Computer Terms in English
and Spanish

Part 2   Sentences in English

Part 3   Computer Terms, Data,
and Word Processing Terms

INTRODUCTION

Computer technology is no longer the province of the technical experts. A whole vocabulary of specialized terms has invaded practically every business and organizational operation throughout the world. With the advent of the home computer, many of these terms are already part of our everyday speech.

The explosion of knowledge accompanying the technological advances is difficult for the non-specialist to keep up with. Nevertheless, we are all faced today with the challenge to become familiar with and to use correctly the "new" language that is constantly being utilized to communicate the on-going technological development.

Since the computer vocabulary in its specialized meanings is still acquiring new terms, this chapter can only serve to introduce the student to a few of the most fundamental vocabulary now universally accepted.

PART 1

DEFINITIONS IN ENGLISH AND SPANISH

Terms	Definitions in English and Spanish
1. APL (A program-ming lan-guage)	A programming language designed to solve mathematical problems. Its brevity is its main characteristic. Lenguaje de Programación diseñado para resolver problemas matemáticos, caracterizado por su brevedad.
2. Basic	It is the beginners' all purpose symbolic instruction code. A high-level language used in most personal computers and fairly easy for beginners to learn. It is the most popular computer language. Lenguaje para principiantes. Basic es un lenguaje de alto nivel que se usa en la mayoría de las computadoras personales. También es fácil para los principiantes aprenderlo. Es el más popular de los lenguajes de computadoras.
3. Cobol	Common business-oriented language. One of the best languages for doing business data processing. A strong point favoring Cobol is its ability to handle a vast amount of data. Es uno de los mejores lenguajes para usar en el procesamiento de data comercial. Un punto fuerte que favorece a Cobol es su habilidad para bregar con enormes cantidades de data.

4. Computer

A machine with a logic center, a memory, a controllable unit and a means for getting data into and out of it.

Es una máquina que tiene un centro de lógica, una memoria, una unidad de control y un medio para obtener datos o para introducirlos en ella.

5. Data Base

A collection of data files containing information material on a particular subject.

Banco de datos o de información que contiene información sobre un tema en particular.

6. Floppy

A plastic magnetic record or disk used to store large amounts of information. It is also called a "floppy" disk. It is called "floppy" because it is thin and flexible.

Record o disco plástico y magnético que se usa para almacenar grandes cantidades de información. Se le llama "floppy" por que es fino y flexible. A veces se le llama "diskette".

7. Fortran (Acronym for Formula Translator)

Acronym for Formula Translator. It is a high-level programming language developed for mathematical operations required by scientists and engineers.

Es un lenguaje de programación de alto nivel, desarrollado para resolver los problemas matemáticos que los científicos e ingenieros enfrentan.

8. Hardware

In computer terms, hardware includes the computer, printers, storage devices and any add-on equipment.

En términos de computadoras, "hardware" incluye la computadora, sus aparatos de almacenaje y cualquier otro equipo que se le quiera añadir.

9. High-level
   language

A programming language such as Basic, written in a kind of English shorthand rather than in numbers and symbols. Algol, Basic, Fortran and Pascal are examples of high-level languages.

Lenguaje de alto nivel. Es un lenguaje de programación escrito en inglés sencillo en vez de números y símbolos. Algol, Basic, Fortran y Pascal son lenguajes de alto nivel.

10. Interest Worlds

Areas of special interest for which the computer can serve as a tool or laboratory. Some of these are: music, mathematics, art, language and physics.

Areas de especial interés, a las cuales la computadora puede servir de laboratorio; por ejemplo: música, matemáticas, arte, lenguaje y física.

11. Memory

The memory is the most important resource of a computer. It determines the complexity as well as the number of different programs that can be executed at the same time.

La memoria es el recurso más importante de la computadora. Determina tanto la complejidad como el número de diferentes programas que pueden ser ejecutados a la vez.

12. Micro-
    processor

It is the brain of any computer because it calculates the logical and mathematical operations necessary for the functioning of a computer system.

Este es el cerebro de cualquier computadora porque hace las operaciones lógicas y matemáticas necesarias para el funcionamiento de un sistema de computadora.

13. Modem

An accesory to connect the computer to the telephone.

Un accesorio que conecta a la computadora con el teléfono.

14. Program	A series of instructions given to the computer to perform specific functions. Programa. Lista de instrucciones que le indica a la computadora que realice una labor específica de procesamiento.
15. Rom (Read Only Memory)	Permanent data storage device that once programmed, cannot be reprogrammed. Pastilla de memoria permanente para almacenamiento de programas, las instrucciones y la información o ambas. Esta no se puede alterar en ningún momento.
16. Software	Instructions, manuals, and programs that tell the computer the desired operations to be performed. Software. Instrucciones, manuales, y programas que indican a la computadora las operaciones que debe ejecutar.
17. Store	To place data, instructions or programs in the computer for using them later. Almacenar data, instrucciones o programas en la computadora para usarlos luego.
18. Translator	A program that changes a group of statements in one language into similar statements in another language. Un programa que cambia un grupo de manifestaciones en cierto lenguaje a otro grupo similar en diferente lenguaje.
19. Volatile memory	Memory that does not retain its information content when the switch is turned off. La memoria que no retiene el contenido de su información una vez se le desconecta el botón de la electricidad.

20. Word Proce-
    ssing System

A combination of specific people, procedures, methods, and equipment designed to accomplish transition and distribution of written verbal and recorded work.

Una combinación de personas específicas, procedimientos, métodos y equipo destinado a llevar a cabo la transición y distribución de trabajos grabados, orales y escritos.

PART 2

SENTENCES IN ENGLISH

Using your dictionary, translate the following sentences carefully.

1. The engineer is taking a course in Fortran to ensure more exactness in mathematical operations.

2. If you decide to update your hardware, please let us know. You will see that our prices are very reasonable.

3. Programs written in high-level language are easy to understand.

4. All the computers come with 64k of user memory.

5. The memory is the principal working place of a computer, since all processing takes place in the memory.

6. If the manager buys a modem, we shall be able to make better use of the computer.

7. In some computers, the software includes advanced user-friendly programs for all types of banking, accounting, and business managment.

8. APL (a programming language) requires a special keyboard.

9. There is a new school in San Juan that offers a course which enables the beginner students to use Basic in computer calculations.

10. Cobol was designed to serve business needs rather than to make program development convenient for programming.

11. Many people buy computers to produce their own newsletters and magazines.

12. If the Data Base contains the information you desire, we shall send it to you within two days.

13. Today, more and more companies are relying on convenient floppy disks to record, store and safeguard information.

14. The information that I shall read in ROM will help me in the preparation of a program.

15. Mr. Lema is an expert who can handle the operational and technical aspects of our micro-processors.

16. The typist must master the basic language skills, such as correct spelling, grammar, and punctuation in order to produce documents of high quality.

17. The will was held in storage until the lawyer and the testator were ready to discuss certain changes.

18. The word processing system stimulates the members of an organization to develop skills that benefit both the organization and the employees.

19. There is much expensive accounting software written specifically for certain computer trademarks.

20. Some information that can be stored is the format of a project and the body of form letters.

PART 3

COMPUTER TERMS, DATA AND
WORD PROCESSING TERMS

The following are computer, data processing, and word processing terms. As you will notice, the majority of these are known to you but they have acquired a new context in the computer world.

With the help of your dictionary, write a sentence in English which illustrates the familiar meaning of each term.

Term	Definition in English and Spanish
1. abort	To stop or cancel a procedure or selection in progress.
	Paralizar o cancelar un procedimiento o selección que está en progreso.
2. access	Ability to obtain data from and/ or place it into memory.
	Recuperar o hacer uso de información de un archivo. Se pueden accesar los discos, las memorias, las impresoras.
3. address	An identification for a register or location in storage, represented by a name, label, or number.
	Identificación de un registro en el sistema de almacenaje. Esta consiste de: nombre, etiqueta o número.
4. back up	Duplication of a program or file stored in separate storage me-

dium; thus, a copy will be kept
against possible loss or damage
to the original.

Duplicado de un programa o ficha.
Se reserva para casos de urgencia
(pérdida o daño del original), y está
en almacenaje separado.

5. bug

A mistake, malfunction or defect
in any part of the computer, program or system.

Error, mal funcionamiento del com-
putador, programa o sistema.

6. debugging

Remove errors or malfunctions
from the computer.

Depurar, corrección del programa
o del equipo cuando no está fun-
cionando en forma adecuada.

7. data
   dictionary

Among other uses, it can be used to
determine a possible change in the
data, and how this change could affect
other programs.

Diccionario de datos. Se puede
utilizar para determinar un posible cambio en los datos y como
éstos afectarían todos los programas.

8. entity

Entity is whatever an organization
wants to describe. This can be a
policy, a will, or a client, etc.

Una entidad es lo que una organi-
zación desee describir. Esto puede
ser una póliza, un testamento, un
cliente, etc.

9. test data

Test data is used to prove and
debug programs. It must have
plenty of convincing proof in
order to be able to prove the
program completely.

Los datos de prueba se usan para
eliminar errores en los programas.
Debe haber suficientes datos convincentes de prueba para así poder

determinar si el programa está
bien.

10. user friendly   Software and hardware systems that
are easy to learn to operate. The
user doesn't need any specialized
training.

Sistemas de "software" y "hardware"
que son fáciles de aprender a operar. El usuario no necesita pre-
paración especializada.

GLOSSARIES

GLOSSARY

THIS ABRIDGED GLOSSARY IS INTENDED ONLY FOR THE SPECIFIC MATERIAL USED IN THIS TEXTBOOK.

PART I

abridge (v.)	acortar, abreviar, privar, despojar
abrogate (v.)	abrogar, abolir
accrued (adj.)	acumulado, devengado
accrued interest	intereses acumulados
accrued vacation	vacaciones acumuladas
acting (adj.)	suplente, interino
acting manager	administrador interino
.acting executive director	director ejecutivo interino
actual (adj.)	real, legítimo
actual value	valor en el mercado
actual price	precio verdadero
address (v.)	hablar a, dirigir la palabra a
adept (adj.)	experto, versado (en)
adjourn (v.)	aplazar, diferir, suspender una sesión
adjourn the hearing	suspender la vista
adjourn a session	levantar la sesión
adjust (v.)	ajustar, arreglar, componer, corregir
adjust an account	ajustar una cuenta
admit (v.)	admitir, recibir, dar entrada
admit (ted) to the bar	recibirse de abogado
admonish (v.)	reprender, amonestar
alienate (v.)	enemistar, alejar, antagonizar
apply (v.)	aplicar
apply color	aplicar color
apply for a job	solicitar un empleo
apply on account	acreditar a la cuenta
appraisal	apreciación, evaluación
appraiser	tasador, evaluador
appropriation (n.)	asignación, consignación
appropriation commitee	comisión o comité de asignaciones
asset (n.)	activo, haber, todo lo que tiene una persona de valor, (fig) ventaja

audit (v.)	intervenir, revisar, ajustar las cuentas
bankruptcy (n.)	bancarrota, quiebra
referee in *bankruptcy*	juez de quiebras, árbitro de quiebras
bargain (n.)	convenio, pacto, ganga
bargain (v.)	pactar, concertar, regatear
bargain away	vender demasiado barato
bear (v.)	llevar, cargar, soportar, producir, rendir, devengar
bear interest	devengar interés
beginning (n.)	comienzo, principio, origen
beginning inventory	inventario de entrada o inicial
bequeath	legar, dejar en testamento
board	consejo, junta
bond (n.)	lazo, vínculo, obligación, bono
in *bond*	en depósito como fianza
bond (adj.)	depositado como fianza, dado en garantía
bonded warehouse	depósito de aduana
bottleneck (n.)	obstrucción, dificultad ,embotellamiento,
brand	marca
brand goods	artículos de marca
bring about	causar, originar
brisk (adj.)	vivo, activo
broker (n.)	corredor, cambista, agente
exchange *broker*	corredor de cambio
investment *broker*	corredor de títulos rentables
real estate *broker*	corredor de bienes raíces
stock broker	corredor de acciones
brochure (n.)	folleto
by-product	producto derivado, secundario
carry	cargar
carry on business with	tener negocios con
carry in stock	tener en existencia
carte blanche (n.)	poder incondicional, carta blanca
ceiling (n.)	techado, cielo raso
ceiling prices	precios máximos fijados por ley
challenge (v.)	desafiar, retar
challenge the accusation	retar la acusación
change (v.)	mudar, cambiar, alterar
change hands	cambiar de dueño
charge (n.)	carga, obligación, precio, gasto
custom *charges*	gastos de aduana
prepaid *charges*	gastos pagados por adelantado
shipping *charges*	gastos de embarque
chattels	bienes muebles
clear (v.)	saldar

clear accounts	saldar cuentas
close (v.)	cerrar, unir, juntar
close a transaction	cerrar una transacción
cogent (adj.)	fuerte, patente, convicente
contract (n.)	contrato
breach of *contract*	incumplimiento de contrato
collection (n.)	colección, cobro, recaudación
commendable (adj.)	loable, digno de alabanza
commensurate (adj.)	proporcionado, comensurado
commensurate with	equivalente a, en proporción con, proporcionado a
consignee (n.)	destinatario
conscientious (adj.)	escrupuloso, recto, concienzudo
container (n.)	envase, recipiente
cardboard *container*	envases de carton
contempt (n.)	desprecio, desdén, menosprecio
contempt of court	desacato (a la autoridad del tribunal)
contend (v.)	sostener, afirmar, asegurar
contest (v.)	impugnar, atacar, competir
contingency (n.)	contingencia, eventualidad, caso imprevisto
contingent	contingente, eventual
contingent upon	depender de
conveyance	escritura de traspaso, transporte
means of *conveyance*	medios de transporte, comunicación
corporate seal	sello de la corporación
costume (n.)	traje, vestido, disfraz
costume jewelry	joyería de fantasía
crowded (adj.)	atestado, abarrotado, hacinamiento
curb (v.)	refrenar, contener, reprimir
current (adj.)	actual, corriente, de actualidad
cut	reducir, cortar
cut expenses	reducir gastos
deadline (n.)	fecha límite
debt (n.)	deuda, débito, obligación
bad *debt*	deuda incobrable
defendant	acusado, demandado
default	falta, ausencia, incumplimiento (de pago) en rebeldia
defray (v.)	costear, sufragar, pagar
delivery (n.)	liberación, entrega, dicción
home *delivery*	entrega a domicilio
deplete (v.)	agotar, mermar
disbar (v.)	desaforar, expulsar del foro
disbarment (n.)	desaforo, expulsión del foro

disclose (v.)	revelar, divulgar
discount (n.)	descuento
quantity *discount*	descuento por comprar en grandes cantidades
dividend	dividendo, cuota proporcional de ganancia
domestic (adj.)	nativo, doméstico, nacional
domestic commodities	artículos o productos nacionales, del país
dormant (adj.)	inactivo
dormant merchandise	mercancía que no se vende
draw (v.)	retirar, devengar
draw a check in favor of	extender un cheque a favor de
draw on a person	girar en contra de una persona
draw back (v.)	retroceder
drawback (n.)	revés, inconveniente, atraso, impedimento, desventaja
drop (v.)	abandonar, descender, caer
drop in price	baja en precio
duty (n.)	deber, tarea, impuesto, derechos de aduana
duty free	libre de impuesto
earmark (v.)	marcar de manera distintiva, separar dinero para un fin especial
enforce (v.)	dar fuerza, forzar, obligar
enforce the law	poner en vigor la ley
envelope (n.)	sobre, cubierta, envoltura
envelope moistener	humedecedor de sobres
eviction (n.)	desahucio
exemplary	ejemplar
exemplary behavior	conducta, ejemplar
exchange (n.)	cambio, cange
in *exchange* for	a cambio de
an *exchange* on the purchase	cambio de la mercancía comprada
expedite (v.)	dar curso a, expedir, acelerar, apresurar
export (n.)	exportación
export customer	cliente en mercados exteriores
export duties	derechos sobre exportaciones
extend (v.)	extender, otorgar, dar
courtesies *extended* to a person	atenciones brindadas a una persona
fall due	vencerse (la nota, letra, préstamo, pagaré, etc.)
far (adv.)	lejos, a distancia)

far reaching project	proyecto de mucho alcance, trascendental
feasible (adj.)	factible, posible
figure (v.)	figurarse, imaginarse, figurar
figure out	estimar o calcular
file (v.)	presentar, archivar
file a complaint	presentar una denuncia o queja
fill (v.)	llenar, cumplimentar
fill an order	servir o cumplimentar un pedido
firm (n.)	empresa, compañía
firm name	razón social, firma
flaw (n.)	imperfección, defecto, falta, falla
foodstuff (n.)	alimentos, comestibles, víveres
foreclose (v.)	ejecutar una hipoteca
foreign (adj.)	extranjero, exterior
foreign market	mercado extranjero
forge	falsificar, contrahacer
forsee (v.)	prever
forward (v.)	enviar, remitir, despachar
forward the goods	enviar la mercancía
freeze (v.)	congelar
freeze assets	congelar activos
freeze jobs	congelar empleos
freeze ceiling prices	congelar precios máximos
freight (n.)	carga, flete
freight rates	tarifas de flete
fringe benefits	beneficios marginales o suplementarios
from (prep.)	de, desde, por
from memory	de memoria
full (adj.)	completo, abundante, detallado
full pay	paga completa
gratifying (adj.)	grato satisfactorio, magnífico
ground	tierra, suelo, territorio
lose ground	perder terreno
handle (v.)	manejar, tratar, comerciar en
handle exclusively	trabajar exclusivamente
handle the matter	atender o bregar con el asunto
haulage (n.)	arrastre, acarreo
head (n.)	cabeza, jefe
head of a business	jefe de un negocio
department *head*	jefe de departamento
hold (v.)	agarrar, defender, detener
hold up the order	detener el pedido
honor (v.)	honrar, aceptar, venerar
honor a draft	aceptar un giro

honor a check	aceptar un cheque
inmates (n.)	reclusos, confinados
impend (v.)	amenazar, ser inminente
imprint (v.)	imprimir, estampar
imprinted checks	cheques impresos
inflate (v.)	soplar, hinchar, inflar
installment plan	plan de pago, facilidades de pago pago a plazos
itemize (v.)	detallar, particularizar
itemized invoice	factura detallada
jeopardy (n.)	peligro, riesgo
in *jeopardy*	en peligro
jeopardize (v.)	comprometer, exponer, arriesgar
joint (v.)	unión, articulación
joint account	cuenta conjunta, cuenta mancomunada
joint obligation	obligación solidaria
keep (v.)	mantener, conservar, cuidar
keep down expenses	reducir gastos
keep on file	mantener en archivo
keep the books	llevar los libros de contabilidad
landlord	arrendador, propietario
lapse	prescribir, quedar interrumpida, caducar
labor turnover	cambio de personal obrero
lay(v.)	extender, proyectar, exhibir, depositar
lay out the plans	exponer los planes
lead (v.)	guiar, conducir, inducir, influenciar
lead astray	descarriar, distraer, seducir
lease	contrato de arrendamiento
leak (v.)	escurrirse, dejar escapar
leak out (fig.)	trascender, divulgarse
lagacy (n.)	legado, herencia
levy	recaudar, exigir
levy taxes	imponer contribuciones
liabilities	pasivo, desventaja, riesgo
likelihood	probabilidad, posibilidad
liquidate (a business)	liquidar un negocio
maintenance (n.)	mantenimiento, manutención
maintenance costs	gastos de conservación
maintenance crew	personal de mantenimiento

make	hacer
make room for	hacer lugar para
match (v.)	aparear, igualar, ser iguales, hacer juego con
matter	materia con que se hace algo, cuestión asunto u objeto de que se trata
as the *matter* stands	según la situación
mature (v.)	vencer, cumplirse el plazo
maturity (n.)	madurez, edad madura, vencimiento
maturity date	fecha de vencimiento
maturity value	valor al vencimiento
meet quarterly payments	hacer frente a pagos trimestrales
merge (v.)	unirse, fusionarse, juntarse
merit (v.)	merecer, ser digno de
merit one's confidence	merecer la confianza de uno
mislead (v.)	extraviar, perder, engañar
misleading advertisements	anuncios engañosos (que confunden)
move (v.)	mudar, impulsar, promover
move in	mudarse a una casa
move out	mudarse de una casa
moving (n.)	movimiento, mudanza, conmovedor
moving van	camión, carro de mudanza
narrow (v.)	limitar (en extensión)
account (n.)	cuenta, causa, motivo
on *account* of	a causa de
open (v.)	abrir, iniciar, hacer accesible
open an account	abrir una cuenta
open (ing) phrases	palabras preliminares
out	fuera
out of stock	no tener en existencia
outstanding	destacado, pendiente de pago, sin cobrar
outstanding account	cuenta pendiente de pago
outstanding checks	cheques no cobrados
outward	exterior, externo, aparente
outward freight	cargamento o flete de ida
overdraw (v.)	sobregirar, exceder su giro
overdrawn account	cuenta sobregirada
overhead	elevado, colgante
overhead expenses	gastos generales de administración
oversight (n.)	equivocación, descuido involuntario
packing (v.)	empaquetar, embalar
packing season	temporada de embalaje

pay (n.)	paga
take home *pay*	sueldo después de las deducciones, sueldo neto
purchasing power	poder de adquisición
perishable (adj.)	frágil, perecedero
perishable goods	mercancías de fácil descomposición. perecedera
pioneer (v.)	iniciar, promover
plaintiff	demandante
power (n.)	poder, dominio
power of attorney	poder, procuración
pressing (adj.)	apremiante, urgente
pressing matter	negocio o asunto urgente
price tag (n.)	etiqueta o marbete de precio
prohibitory (adj.)	prohibitorio
promissory note (n.)	pagaré
protracted (adj.)	largo, lento
proxy (n.)	poder, procuración delegación
by *proxy*	por poder
marry by *proxy*	casarse por poder
quantity (n.)	cantidad
quantity discount	descuento por comprar en grandes cantidades
quarterly (adj.)	trimestral
quarterly payment	pago trimestral
qualified (adj.)	calificado, idóneo, apto, competente
quote (n.)	cita, cotización
rate (n.)	tasa, valuación, tipo, tarifa
rate of exchange	tipo de cambio
realize (v.)	darse cuenta, reconocer, realizar efectuar
recur (v.)	repetirse, volver a presentarse en la memoria
recurrence (n.)	reaparición, repetición
refund (v.)	reembolsar, devolver
release (v.)	aflojar, liberar
release the order	dar curso al pedido
release on parole	poner en libertad bajo palabra
retailer (n.)	comerciante al por menor
reimburse (v.)	reembolsar, reintegrar

reinstate (v.)	reinstalar, reintegrar, restablecer
reluctant (adj.)	reacio, renuente
with *reluctancy*	a regañadiente, de mala gana
replenish (v.)	reaprovisionar, proveer
replenish the stock	surtir de nuevo la mercancía agotada
rest (v.)	descansar, confiar, cesar, parar, depender
rest assured	estar seguro, perder cuidado
	tener la seguridad
retail (n.)	menudeo, venta al por menor
retailer (n.)	detallista
right (n.)	derecho, prerrogativa, correcto
right of way	derecho de paso o de tránsito,
	servidumbre de paso
rise (n.)	elevación, altura
rise and fall of prices	alza y baja de precios
running (n.)	corriente, funcionamiento
running expenses (adj.)	*gastos de operación*
sale (n.)	*venta*
sale on a cash basis	venta de contado
schedule (n.)	programa, lista, inventario,
	horario (de trenes, aviones, etc)
schedule (v.)	proyectar, fijar el tiempo o la hora de
scramble (n.)	contienda, lucha, hacer esfuerzos
	para alcanzar algo, huevos revueltos
securities (n.)	valores, títulos
service (n.)	servicio, ayuda, asistencia
service station	puesto o estación surtidora de gasolina
setback (n.)	contrariedad, revés
settle (v.)	establecer, aclarar, ajustar
settle an account	arreglar (cuentas), saldar una cuenta
settlement (n.)	ajuste, colonización, saldo,
	liquidación
settlement of the estate	partición de la herencia
share (v.)	compartir, participar de
share (n.)	acción, parte
short (adj.)	escaso, reducido, limitado
short of	escaso de
signatory (n.)	firmante, signatario
situation (n.)	situación, posición
situation forced upon a person	situación impuesta a una persona
skilled workers	trabajadores diestros

slow (adj.)	lento, tardío
slow in payment	lento, moroso al pagar
sole (adj.)	solo, único, exclusivo
solicit (v.)	solicitar, demandar
solicit support	solicitar apoyo
solvent	solvente, con recursos
sort (v.)	apartar, dividir, ordenar
sort the stock	clasificar la mercancía, ponerla en orden
stale (adj.)	añejo, viejo, rancio
stale check	cheque caducado, cheque invalidado por no haberse efectuado su cobro a tiempo
staple (n.)	producto principal de un país
staple commodities	renglones de primera necesidad
statement (n.)	declaración, manifestación
statement of account	estado de cuenta
stem (v.)	provenir, descender
stock (n.)	acciones, inventario, existencia
stock on hand	mercancía en almacén
out of *stock*	no tener mercancía en existencia
stock up (v.)	proveerse de, abastecerse de
straighten (v.)	enderezar, arreglar, ordenar
straighten our accounts	aclarar nuestras cuentas
stringent (adj.)	severo, estricto, riguroso
subject (n.)	sujeto, expuesto
subject to	sujeto a
subsidize (v.)	subvencionar, ayudar económicamente
suitable (adj.)	conforme, conveniente, satisfactorio
suitable prices	precios convenientes, satisfactorios
stockholder (n.)	tenedor de acciones, accionista
take-home pay (n.)	sueldo después de las deducciones
tally (v.)	ajustar, concordar, cuadrar, corresponder
tally accounts	cuadrar cuentas
to keep *tally*	contar, contramarcar, hacer cuadrar
to *tally* votes	llevar cuenta de los votos
tamper-proof (adj.)	a prueba de manoseo, a prueba de alteración
telephone directory (n.)	guía de teléfono
teller (n.)	narrador, cajero (de un banco)), escrutador (de votos)
tenant (n.)	inquilino
testator (n.)	testador

tight money	dinero escaso, difícil de obtener
throw money away	malgastar dinero
trace (v.)	trazar, investigar, rastrear, seguir la pista, averiguar el paradero de
tracer (n.)	cédula de investigación (cédula que da derecho a que traten de averiguar el paradero de objetos perdidos)
traffic jam (n.)	embotellamiento del tráfico
trial balance	balance de comprobación
under (prep.)	bajo, debajo de
under contract	bajo contrato
under discussion	bajo condición
undersell (v.)	vender a bajo precio, baratear
underrate (v.)	menospreciar, subestimar, rebajar
underwriter (n.)	asegurador, compañía aseguradora
upon (prep.)	sobre, encima, de, en, a
upon your arrival	a su llegada
upkeep (n.)	conservación, mantenimiento
upkeep expenses	gastos de conservación, mantenimiento
use (v.)	emplear, utilizar, consumir
used up (adj.)	agotado, avejentado
utilities (n.)	servicios (agua, luz, etc.)
validate (v.)	validar, dar validez legal a una cosa
van (n.)	furgón
void (adj)	nulo, sin valor, sin fuerza legal,
void (v.) (n.)	anular, invalidar, hueco, vacío
waybill (n.)	hoja de ruta, itinerario
wear (n.)	gasto, deterioro natural,desgaste
wear and tear	desgaste o deterioro debido al uso
well-timed (adj.)	a tiempo oportuno
wholesaler (n.)	vendedor al por mayor
withdraw (n.)	retirar, apartar, remover, retractarse
withdraw quotations	retirar cotizaciones
within (prep.)	dentro de, en el interior de, en el espacio de, al alcance de
within a short distance	a poca distancia
within his income	dentro del límite de sus ingresos
without (prep.)	falto de, sin
without delay	lo más pronto posible, sin demora

would-be (adj.)	pretendiente, aspirante
would-be employees	empleados potenciales
yield (v.)	producir, rendir, ceder, consentir
yield a profit	dar o rendir un beneficio
yield the floor	ceder la palabra

PART II
SPANISH TO ENGLISH

abogar (v.)	to defend, to plead for
abrogar (v.)	repeal, abolish, annul
acarreo (n.)	cartage
a corta distancia	within a short distance
agradeceremos (v.)	we shall appreciate
adhesiones (n.)	adhesion, support
aduana (n.)	customs
afrontar (v.)	to face
ajustarse a nuestras necesidades futuras	conform to our future needs
alzas y bajas	ups and downs
andamiaje (n.)	scaffolding
apelar (v.)	appeal
archivo (n.)	file
artículos de marca	brand-name goods
artículos de primera necesidad	staple commodities
azotar (v.)	beat, strike
bajo ningún concepto	on no account
cargos (n.)	charges
cargos de aduana	customs charges
cargos de embalaje	packing charges
cargos de embarque	shipping charges
cargos de exportación	export duties (charges)
ceder (v.)	yield, surrender
ceder la palabra	yield the floor
cédula (n.)	certificate, order
cédula de investigación	tracer
coartar (v.)	limit, restrain, abridge
cobro (n.)	collection

recordatorio de *cobro*	collection reminder
comité de escrutinio	tellers committee
contingencia (n.)	contingency
contingente (n.)	contingent
convincente (adj.)	convincing, cogent
corredor (n.)	broker
corredor de bienes raíces	real-estate broker
cotejar (v.)	tally, check
cuello azul	blue collar
darse cuenta de	realize
derivado (n.)	by-product, derivative
derrotar la moción	vote down the motion
desgracia (n.)	misfortune, bad luck, disfavor
estar en *desgracia*	to be out of favor
detallado (adj.)	itemized
detallar (v.)	itemize, detail
deterioro natural	wear and tear
devengar (v.)	produce (interest)
diestro (adj.)	skilled, skillful
disipar sus dudas	dispel your doubts
distancia (n.)	distance
a corta *distancia*	within a short distance
engañosos (adj.)	deceiving, misleading
anuncios *engañosos*	misleading advertisements
estado (n.)	statement, account
estado de situación	income report, balance sheet
espectador (n.)	bystander
estación de gasolina	gas station
estancar	to come to a standstill, paralyzed, held up
estibador (n.)	stevedore
etiqueta de precio	price tag
existencia (n.)	goods, stock
en *existencia*	in stock
existencia disponible	stock on hand
existencia en demasía	surplus stock
renovar la *existencia*	to restock
factible (adj.)	feasible
filtrar (v.) (divulgación no autorizada de noticias	leak
gastos (n.)	expenses
gastos de embalaje	packing expenses

gastos de flete	freight expenses
gastos generales	overhead expenses
gastos de operación	running expenses
gerente (n.)	manager
gerente interino	acting manager
gerente de mantenimiento	maintenance manager
gastar (v.)	spend, disburse
gastar en exceso de lo que se gana	live beyond one's income
hacinamiento (n.)	crowded conditions
honrar (v.)	accept, pay
idóneo (adj.)	suitable, proper, apt
imponer (v.)	to impose, levy
impugnar (v.)	to contradict, refute, to contest
inminente (adj.)	impending
inventario (n.)	inventory
inventario de entrada	beginning inventory
loable (adj)	commendable, praiseworthy
mantener en archivo	to keep on file
merma (n.)	decrease, reduction
pesquisa (n.)	inquest, investigation
peatón (n.)	pedestrian
poder	power
poder absoluto	absolute power, carte blanche
poder adquisitivo	purchasing power
poner en peligro	jeopardize
pléyade (n.)	number of... (figurative)
precios máximos	ceiling prices
poner en vigor	enforce
préstamos (n.)	loans
préstamos a corto plazo	short-term loans
presupuesto (n.)	budget
presupuesto de largo alcance	far-reaching budget
proporción	proportion
en *proporción* con	in proportion with, commensurate with
productos (n.)	products
productos de primera necesidad	staples
rastrear (v.)	track, trace
reclusos o confinados	inmates

reducir (v.)	reduce, cut down
reducir los gastos	cut down expenses
reembolso (n.)	refund, reimbursement
reinstalar	reinstate
remolque (n.)	towage
renuente	reluctant
repartición (n.)	distribution
repartición de la herencia	settlement of the estate
sobregirar (v.)	overdraw
solicitar (v.)	solicit, apply
solicitar apoyo	solicit support
subestimar (v.)	underrate
subvencionar (v.)	subsidize
talonario de cheque	check stub
tarea especial	part-time
tomar prestado a	borrow from
traer a colación	make mention of, bring up
trimestral (adj)	quarterly
vacío (n.)(v.)	void (n.), unoccupied, vacant
víveres (n.)	foodstuffs, victuals

SELECTED REFERENCE BIBLIOGRAPHY
General

Bander, Robert G. *American English Rhetoric*, 2nd. ed., Holt, Rinehart and Winston, Inc., New York, 1978.

Barnstein, Diane B. *An Introduction to Transformational Grammar*, Winthrop Publishers, Inc., Cambridge, Mass., 1977.

Contrastive Linguistics and Its Pedagogical Implications, James E. Alatis, ed., Monograph Series on Languages and Linguistics no. 21, Georgetown University Press, Washington, D.C., 1968.

Escobar, Dagget and Savariego. *Bilingual Skills for Commerce and Industry and Guide for Translators*, Southwestern Publishing Co., Cincinnati, Ohio, U.S.A., 1984.

Gleason , H.A. *Linguistics and English Grammar*, Holt, Rinehart and Winston, Inc., New York, 1965.

Hendry, J.F. *Your Future in Translating and Interpreting*, Richards Press, Inc., New York, 1969.

Hughes, John P. *Linguistics and Language Teaching*, Random House, New York, 1968.

Nida, Eugene A. *Toward a Science of Translating*, E.J. Brill, Leiden, Holland, 1964.

Stockwell, R.P., Bowen, J.D., and Martin, John W. *The Grammatical Structures of English and Spanish*, Contrastive Structure Series, Charles A. Ferguson, General Editor, University of Chicago Press, Chicago, 1965.

The World of Translation, Papers delivered at the Conference on Literary Translation held in New York, May, 1970, under the auspices of PEN American Center, Congrat-Butler, New York, 1971.

Translations Register-Index (1967), Guide to Reference Books, Constance M. Winchell, ed., American Library Association, Chicago, 1967.

DICTIONARIES

Chamber's Technical Dictionary, C.F. Tweney, ed., 3rd. ed.rev., The Macmillan Company, New York, 1958.

Collin's Spanish Dictionary: Spanish-English / English-Spanish, William Collin's Sons and Co., London and Glasgow, 1971.

Diccionario de la Lengua Española Real Academia Española, Editorial Espasa Calpe, S.A. Carretera de Irún, Km. 12,200, Madrid, 1984.

Dictionary of American Idioms, Adam Mackae, ed., Barron's Educational Series, Inc., New York, 1975.

Dictionary of Technical Terms, Frederic S. Crispin, ed., 9th ed. rev., Brace, Milwaukee, 1961.

Fowler, H.W. *A Dictionary of Modern English Usage*, 2nd. ed., revised and edited by Sir Ernest Gowers, Oxford University Press, New York, 1965.

Freedman, Alan, *Glosario de Computación*, 3rd. ed., Libros de McGraw Hill de Mexico, Tipografía Barsa, S.A. Mexico, D. F., 1983.

Giordano, Albert G., *Concise Dictionary of Business Terminology*, Prentice Hall, Inc., Englewood Cliffs, New Jersey, 1981.

International Dictionary, Simmon and Schuster, Inc., Rockefeller Center, 630 Fifth Avenue, New York, 1973.

Martínez Amador, Emilio M. *Diccionario gramatical*. Editorial Ramón Sopena, Barcelona, 1954.

Roget's International Thesaurus, 3rd. ed., Thomas Y Crowell Company New York, 1962.

Sáinz de Robles, Federico Carlos, *Ensayo de un diccionario español de sinónimos y antónimos*, Editorial Aguilar, Madrid, 1970.

Savaiano, Eugene and Lynn Wingate. *Spanish and English Idioms*, Barron's Educational Series, Inc., New York, 1976.

The American Heritage Dictionary of the English Language, American Publishing Co. Inc., and Houghton Mifflin Company, Boston, 1971.

The Illustrated Computer Dictionary, Publications International Ltd., 3841 West Oakton Street, Skokie, Illinois, 60076, 1983.

Thesaurus: terminología dinámica de las nuevas técnicas comerciales, Biblioteca de la dirección de empresas, ed., B. Prat Gaballe, Hispano-Europea, Barcelona, 1965.

Webster's Seventh New Collegiate Dictionary, C. and C. Merriam Company, Springfield, Mass., 1971.

Webster's Synonyms, Antonyms, and Homonyms, Ottenheimer Publishers Inc., New York, 1962.

Este libro se terminó de imprimir
en mayo de 1993
en los talleres de
C P I
San Juan, Puerto Rico